When the Country Went to Town

Duff Hart-Davis

When the Country Went to Town

The Countryside Marches and Rally of 1997

EXCELLENT PRESS
LUDLOW

First published in 1997

Excellent Press
Palmers House
7 Corve Street
Ludlow
Shropshire SY8 1DB

ISBN 1 900318 0 67

Printed and Bound by the Cromwell Press,
Broughton Gifford, Melksham,
Wiltshire SN12 8PH

Smile at us, pay us, pass us; but do not quite forget.
For we are the people of England, that never have spoken yet.

G. K. Chesterton, *The Secret People*

Contents

Baroness Mallalieu

On 10 July 1997 the countryside finally came to London to say, 'Enough is enough.' The twin triggers were a new Member of Parliament, with a Private Member's bill to criminalise hunting with hounds, and an apparently unsympathetic new Government.

For some time, and almost invariably with quiet dignity, country men and women have increasingly borne interference, abuse and vilification for activities which they believe to be beneficial to wild animals, to rural communities and to the countryside itself. The attack has almost always come from people who have never had any experience of the day-to-day care and management of animals or the land, or any responsibility for them.

Field sports, and especially hunting, have borne the main force of that abuse, but the attack goes far deeper. It is, quite simply, an assault on the freedom of others to live their lives in ways which you would not wish to lead yours, or in ways which you do not yourself either understand or care for.

It has been said that to those who do not understand hunting, no explanation is possible, and that to those who do, no explanation is necessary. I hope this is not so. To those of us who have heard the music of the hounds and have loved it, it is far more than just a sport. Hunting is our music, it is our poetry, it is our art, it is our pleasure. It is where many of our best friendships are made, it is our community, it is our whole way of life. We will fight for these things with all the strength and dedication we possess, because we love them. The road to Hyde Park was taken by over 120,000 people. The marchers showed the way. In the weeks before the rally those men, women and children who walked so captured the imagination of the nation that the success of the rally was assured, although its scale turned out to be beyond imagining.

But they did more. As they marched, the media focused on them, and for the first time our largely urban and suburban nation began to see the arguments, decency, sincerity and passion of those who cared enough about these things to give up part of their lives. For the first time the real issues began to be examined in the press. Journalists came to see and speak to the marchers, and began to understand. By 10 July the nation could see that these were not the wealthy, privileged stereotypes suggested by the campaigners for abolition, but ordinary people, animal lovers too, with their own experiences, values and backgrounds, who held a different view. Our nation, small though it is, contains many different worlds. The world of the countryman, who cares for his sports, may be a far cry from Islington, but it is at the heart of our nation and its history. To tamper with country freedoms because they are not understood, or are disapproved of by a majority in whose world they have no place, would be to provoke unprecedented anger in a part of our population which is fundamentally decent and law-abiding, and upon whose cooperation and goodwill good government depends. The consequences of interference are not to be contemplated. By the dignity of their protest and the lead they gave, the marchers turned the tide of opinion in favour of the countryside.

CHAPTER ONE

Sparks in the Tinder

At 8.50 am on 27 June 1997 the Welsh Countryside March was about to leave the town of Machynlleth on the first leg of its great trek to London. The junction in front of the clock-tower buzzed with activity as thirty-five core marchers, who were walking all the way, shifted restlessly from foot to foot, testing the fit of their boots. Round the group of bright-yellow T-shirts milled a mass of day-walkers and other supporters, all in a state of nervous anticipation. David Jones, the marchers' leader and Huntsman of the David Davies hounds, was being interviewed for television. A stocky, dark, fine-looking man in his fifties, he was asked what would happen if hunting with hounds were banned. 'I'll tell you straight,' he replied. 'The first casualty would be the red kite. We've spent thousands trying to bring him back, and he'd be wiped from the face of the earth.' He explained that kites, successfully re-introduced to Central Wales during recent years, are scavengers, and that if farmers were deprived of their most efficient means of controlling foxes, they would scatter poison baits, which the hawks would inevitably pick up. Five minutes later, Jones led his men and women off down the High Street, out over a cattle grid and across the golf course on the common. Suddenly, out to his right, he spotted a red kite, three or four hundred yards off. Suspecting that many of the company had never seen one, and would not know what the bird was, he shouted, 'Red kite on the right!' – whereupon the big, lithe raptor, instead of giving the humans a wide berth, dived straight towards the straggling crocodile, came down to within a few feet of it, and flew the length of the column with its head turned to one side as it surveyed the 220-odd marchers. When

1

it reached the last of them, it dipped one wing, lifted away like a fighter aircraft and vanished into the sky. That astonishing, almost supernatural visitation made the hair on David Jones's arms rise up. Never in all his years as a huntsman in the mountains had he seen anything like it. Never in his life had he known a bird behave in such a way. Many of the marchers were shaken by the incident, which became the talk of the day. As Jones remarked later, 'If that wasn't a good omen, what was it?'

Nobody can say who first had the idea of starting a latter-day peasants' revolt – for by the beginning of 1997 discontent had become so widespread that all across the country people were wondering how they might demonstrate their ever-increasing annoyance at the manner in which their jobs, traditions and very way of life were being threatened by the uncomprehending dogmatism of urban politicians. One potential rebel was Chipps Mann, wife of a Gloucestershire farmer, who, as she was driving home on a January evening, abruptly announced to a friend, 'I'm going to walk from Cornwall to London.' Although the notion smouldered on in her mind, she did not take a train to Penzance for the time being. Instead, on 15 January, during a spell of hard weather, she wrote to the *Field* and other country magazines a letter which began:

> Being the only non-hunting member of my family, I have been asking myself recently, during this long abstention from hunting due to the frost, why I would fight tooth and nail to prevent the Labour Party, or an ignorant Conservative Government, from banning this, the first of many field sports . . .
> The answer is, apart from hating change for change's sake, that it would be change brought about by ignorance and fashion. On the whole those in power do not really care about hunting, but it is fashionable to abuse it.

Mrs Mann went on to say that what really worried her was the apathy being shown by those 'whose lives would be irrevocably diminished by a ban on hunting.' Inciting all concerned to take up 'the call to arms', she invited people who found the British Field

Sports Society 'too intimidating' to write to her, 'and I will help you to help them.' By then – mid-January – the idea of staging a major protest was already well advanced at the headquarters of the BFSS in London. Already everyone knew that a General Election would take place by May 1997, at the latest, and a change of Government from Conservative to Labour seemed highly probable, with a consequent intensification of the threat to field sports, fox-hunting in particular. From all over the country members of the Society were ringing and writing to say that they wanted to come to London to make their point: from all quarters they were demanding action, loud and clear.

During the past few years, under its new Chief Executive, the suave and articulate Robin Hanbury-Tenison, the BFSS had made strenuous efforts to improve its defence of field sports. Now, at its palatial headquarters in South London – an elegant, white Victorian building, once the home of the Kennington Town Council, but recently presented to the Society by a benefactor – Hanbury-Tenison and his colleagues considered various options for action. Over Christmas 1996 they had brought in an outsider, Simon Clarke, a former army officer, farmer and huntsman (known in his regiment, The Blues, as 'Badger' Clarke), to act as co-ordinator for whatever scheme they might devise. One idea was to lay on a huge country fair in Hyde Park during the summer of 1997. Then came proposals for a march on Parliament; but the BFSS soon discovered that it is illegal to march on Parliament while the House is sitting – and to march at a time when MPs were absent seemed pointless.

Soon the Society opted for a rally in Hyde Park, but there were protracted arguments about whether the gathering should be held in mid-week or at a weekend. Obviously it would be easier for people to attend on a Saturday or Sunday, and numbers at a mid-week rally might be relatively low. On the other hand, one faction thought that the risk of disruption by antis would be greater at the weekend, and that the rally could end in a bloodbath, which would discredit the whole countryside movement.

In the end, those voting for mid-week won the argument, and a date was chosen. Assuming that there was a change of Government at the beginning of May, it looked as though the first date on which a Private Member's bill could be brought before the House of Commons was Friday, 11 July. Prime Minister's question time was then on Thursdays, and someone suggested that a question should be asked in the House while the rally was in progress. The date selected was therefore Thursday, 10 July.

No immediate announcement was made, but, to gear members up for the big day, the BFSS arranged a series of twenty-three open meetings, at which Hanbury-Tenison went round speaking at provincial centres. These became known as 'Robin's Road-shows', and proved a notable success, attracting 15,000 people overall – an average of over 600 at each. The first took place in Bath on 9 January 1997, but it was not until three weeks later, at a meeting in Cirencester, that Hanbury-Tenison revealed the date, urging everyone present to keep it open.

Meanwhile another pressure group, the Sportsman's Association, was battling to drum up support for the nation's pistol shooters. After the tragedy at Dunblane Primary School, where Thomas Hamilton shot dead a teacher and sixteen pupils on 13 March 1996, the Government had clamped down on hand-guns, and the Association, hurriedly formed in October, held three rallies in Central London to publicise its cause. The first, in December 1996, attracted 4,000 people, who met in Hyde Park and marched to Trafalgar Square, where speeches were made. For the second rally, in January, the total rose to 12,000, and at the third, in February, 22,000 men and women followed the same route.

Among the crowd that day were Simon Clarke and his newly-recruited secretary, twenty-four-year-old Mary Eames. They enjoyed the march, especially when a well-endowed young woman leant from an upper window of the Ritz Hotel, displaying her all, and drew loud cheers from the passing column. As Clarke put it afterwards, 'There was a buzz about the event, and at the BFSS we realised that was what we would have to create if we held a rally of our own.' Next day, however, he was dismayed to find that the demonstration received minimal press coverage: tiny, single-column reports in the *Times* and *Daily Telegraph*, and a little bit more in the *Daily Mail*.

Out in Gloucestershire, Charles and Chipps Mann had exactly the same emotions. Both are in their forties, and behind their

4

cheerful, easy-going demeanour lies steely determination. They had been discussing possible moves with Sam Butler, grandson of the politician Rab Butler, an estate agent and keen hunting man (Joint Master of the Warwickshire), who lived nearby and had known the Manns for years.

Mann and Butler had also joined the Sportsman's rally in February, and thought it brilliantly organised. When they looked back along Piccadilly and realised that half the thoroughfare was a solid mass of marchers, as far as they could see, they thought, 'Fantastic! This must be bringing London to a halt.' Yet when they slipped out of Trafalgar Square with speeches still in progress, and went round one corner, they found everything perfectly normal. 'London didn't know what was happening,' Mann recalled afterwards. 'We saw that over 20,000 people could march through the streets, and London didn't notice.' They considered this, and the lack of publicity, a disaster, and felt that they themselves could not risk staging a rally if it was going to attract so little attention.

Keen as they were to get some action going, they were still casting about for practical ideas. At that stage their aim was to spread the message about the rally far more widely than to the BFSS's 80,000 members; but their relationship with the Society was uneasy: each side was suspicious of the other, and on 17 February Mann drafted a letter to Simon Clarke which began:

Dear Simon,
Thankyou for your time on the telephone yesterday. We are very keen to be seen not as 'loose cannons' but as wanting to help and lend enthusiastic support and feed in ideas and recruit suppor-ters. Please bear with us, and we will definitely provide you with your crowds.

In due course the promise of this last sentence was handsomely fulfilled; but at the time the whole paragraph seemed too antag-onistic, and Mann dropped it from his letter, which offered co-operation in general terms, and stressed that in any initiative the 'countryside aspect' must be emphasised, because if a rally were seen to be for hunting only, many people would be alienated:

We take your point that discussing the possibility of a rally presumes a Labour victory at the election. However, talking to people on the ground and judging by the reaction in the hall when Robin announced the rally, everyone is so fired up that it would be a big mistake to retract now. People feel we have many enemies in the Conservative Party, and whichever party wins the election needs to be shown the immense strength of feeling in the countryside. We feel the time is right to be *proactive*, not wait until it is nearly too late again and be *reactive*.

Together with Sam Butler and his wife Amanda, the Manns then went skiing, and when they returned home on Easter Sunday, 30 March, they found their answerphone tape full of messages from Mark Miller Mundy, a portrait photographer with whom they had had several conversations before they departed on holiday. Now on the tape he was saying, 'Ring me! Ring me! You must ring me.'

A soft-spoken, mildly-eccentric looking man, with a mop of wiry grey curls, Miller Mundy had never ridden to hounds; but he too was passionately keen that country people should stand up for their rights. For some time he had been casting about in search of practical schemes, and now he thought he had had a brainwave: that people should speak with their feet by marching to London from all corners of the kingdom. Naturally he was longing to discuss ways of putting the idea into practice.

At last he re-established contact with the Manns, and during the next few days he several times drove over for supper at their farmhouse. There the seed of his plan fell into exceptionally fertile ground. Everyone was immediately enthusiastic; everyone wanted to take action. Everyone knew the date of the BFSS's proposed rally. The tenth of July was therefore the *terminus ante quem* – the date by which any countryside march or marches must reach London.

So, by early April, two separate teams were busy with their plans: the BFSS in London, the march organisers in Gloucestershire. All involved were anxious that their protests should be peaceful – and perhaps it was as well that nobody found time to carry out much research into the event with which people began glibly comparing the new initiatives – the Peasants' Revolt of 1381.

That bloody uprising was a protest against excessive taxation, and in particular against that familiar-sounding levy, the poll tax. It began in May, when violence broke out in Essex; then in Kent a crowd marched through Rochester and Maidstone, burning official records. When the rebels reached London in June, led by the rough military adventurer Wat Tyler, they threw the city into confusion. Two leading members of the governing Council, the Archbishop of Canterbury and the Treasurer, were beheaded on Tower Hill; John of Gaunt's Savoy Palace was burnt. But at Smithfield the young king, 14-year-old Richard II, came out to face the rebel leaders.

Their basic demands were for lower taxes and greater freedom: in particular, they claimed that no man ought to be a serf. All might have remained peaceful, had not Tyler showed excessive familiarity with the boy-monarch, shaking his arm roughly and whispering in his ear. The king apparently told him that most of his demands would met, and then ordered him to go back to Kent. A fracas broke out. Tyler was run through with a sword by a yeoman of the King's household, and, though mortally wounded, mounted his horse and rode off for nearly a hundred yards before he fell dying to the ground. His body was carried to the hospital for poor folks at St. Batholemew's; the Mayor of London followed him there, and had him carried back to Smithfield and there decapitated. When Tyler's followers saw his head being carried through the streets on a pole, they begged the King for mercy and melted away. The rebellion rumbled on for several weeks in the country, but in the end the King reneged on his promises of reform, and apart from the abolition of the poll tax, the peasants achieved none of their objectives.

The original Peasants' Revolt, then, was not an encouraging precedent. But also in the minds of the 1997 planners – and far closer in time – was the Jarrow hunger march which took place in the autumn of 1936. Led for much of the way by their Labour Member of Parliament Ellen Wilkinson, 200 shipyard workers walked 300 miles from the Tyne to London, their aim being to draw attention to the plight of their town, where unemployment had reached record levels.

They set out on 5 October and arrived on 1 November. Along the way (according to *The Times*), they were 'greatly cheered by the kindness and hospitality which they received everywhere,' and at the end their leader D.F. Riley – a Jarrow town councillor who walked the entire route in a bowler hat – declared that they were 'three times better men' than when they had started, built up by plenty of good food and exercise, and by 'the moral effect of having something to do every day after prolonged periods of idleness.'

All but three of the starters completed the journey, and when the 197 survivors reached Hyde Park, in a downpour, they were still 'stepping out briskly and cheerfully.' Several thousand people had gathered to welcome them – and it was unfortunate that the London Communist Party had organised a separate rally, demanding an end to the embargo on arms being sent out to Government forces in the Spanish Civil War. But when the Communists realised what was happening, they sportingly lowered their red flag and suspended their own meeting out of sympathy with the men from Jarrow.

The column was to have halted in the park for milk and sandwiches; but because of the rain the men carried on through Mayfair, to the strains of the Minstrel Boy mouth-organ band and the beat of a drum, until they reached Garrick Street, where they had a belated lunch at a soup kitchen. Because of its essential good-humour, the march was hailed as a success; but it achieved very little for the men who had made such an effort.

The third historical precedent was the event in the spring of 1949 which became known as the Piccadilly Hunt. With stag-hunting and coursing under threat from a Private Member's bill, some 400 hunting men hastily arranged a mounted protest in the centre of London. Folk memory claims that some of them took their own horses to town: in fact they went in by bus or train and hired horses from stables in the capital. In those days not everyone was used to road travel. One man, feeling sick in the charabanc, stuck his head out the window to get some fresh air and had his false teeth blown out. Luckily traffic was so light that the driver made a U-turn and the owner collected his lost property without mishap.

In London the ad-hoc cavalcade rode down Piccadilly, agreeably surprised to find that shoppers, taxi-drivers and policemen all seemed to wish them well. Three of the party went on ahead to lobby MPs, and while impassioned debate raged in the House of

Commons, the rest of the company eased their nerves in various hostelries, free of charge. Later that day all were delighted to hear that the bill had been defeated, and ever since then the survivors have held annual reunions to commemorate their victory.

Whether or not the marches and rally of 1997 achieve any political result, only time will show. Early in the year the organisers feared that both projects might go off at half-cock and attract more ridicule than respect. In a few weeks, however, both grew to proportions which far exceeded the planners' initial hopes. Frustration was crackling all over the countryside like dead grass and leaves on the floor of an autumn forest; and as soon as a spark fell into that dry tinder, fire swept through the land.

CHAPTER TWO

Ambassadors for the Countryside

Mark Miller Mundy, also, was puzzled and disappointed by the failure of the Sportsman's Association rally; but on 21 March he happened to meet the editor of a national newspaper, and asked him why the demonstration had achieved so little publicity. The answer was simple. Rallies had become too frequent: they were no longer news. To hit the headlines, the editor told him, some new form of event would be needed.

Realising that another rally would win twenty-four hours' attention at the most, Miller Mundy went away wondering how he could engage the interest of the public over a longer period, so that people would have time to think about the issues involved and express their opinions. He believed that there was 'a huge grass-roots desire to *do* something,' and this made him think of how the out-of-work shipbuilders had marched from Jarrow. His mind turned to marches in general. A large-scale latter-day march would at least give people the chance to demonstrate their anxieties in an active way and get their voices heard.

Although not a hunting man himself, he knew that the fox-hunts maintained by far the most efficient countrywide network of contacts, and he suspected that his best option would be to work through them. So, on the evening of Sunday, 23 March, he telephoned Sir Michael Richardson, Chairman of the Masters of Foxhounds Association (the sport's governing body) and gave an outline of his idea. Richardson, liking the sound of it, asked if he could put something on paper and fax it over. This he did – and that same evening Richardson called back to say that he had circulated the proposal to some of his people, and that their reaction had been very positive.

Miller Mundy was greatly encouraged, because he now felt certain that widespread support would be forthcoming. Next someone told him to make contact with David Jones, who hunts the David Davies hounds in the mountains of Central Wales: a charismatic leader with a wide following, both in his own country and beyond. Over the telephone Jones listened carefully to his exposition and said he would ring back in a couple of days.

Another vital area – Miller Mundy realised – was the north west, where the fell packs hunt on foot, and, as in Wales, chasing foxes is not so much a sport as an essential means of pest-control, and dogs are essential for flushing foxes out of the dense forestry plantations which have grown up since the second world war. He therefore rang Edmund Porter, the quietly-spoken but authoritative Chairman of the Central Committee of Fell Packs, and put the idea of marches to him.

His final ranging call was to David Latham, a Yorkshire farmer who had settled on a small-holding in Cornwall and become Master of the Fulborough Hunt and Chairman of the neighbouring East Cornwall. When Miller Mundy caught Latham on his mobile telephone, he could hear hounds yelping and squeaking in the background, and people talking. He realised that his contact must be on the point of moving off from a meet: nevertheless the two talked for twenty minutes before Latham said he really had to go, and would call back that evening.

Things had started to move at breathtaking speed: it was clear that the grass-roots response was going to be immense. Urgently needed, now, was some organisation which could translate ideas into reality, and an office from which it could work. Charles and Chipps Mann's home near Lechlade was an obvious possibility, for at the back of their farmyard was a range of former pigsties which had been converted into workshops, and one of these might house a few volunteer office staff. Miller Mundy therefore put through several calls to the Manns' number, only to keep getting their answerphone, and he realised belatedly that they must be on holiday.

Then at last, on Tuesday, 1 April, they picked up their messages, answered his appeals and jumped at his idea. At a meeting next day they brought in Sam Butler and introduced him to Miller Mundy.

11

Slim, dark-haired and articulate, Butler was also methodical and efficient – the best possible person to cut half-formed ideas down to size and make them work.

At another planning session, which took place on 8 April, the Manns, Butler and Miller Mundy were joined by Jillie Barrow, first of their volunteer helpers, who delighted them, whenever she gave her name over the telephone, by saying 'Barrow – as in wheelbarrow'. The minutes of the meeting recorded their decisions to call the enterprise 'The Countryside March', to 'encourage all comers', and 'to try to cover all countryside issues.' Office equipment was to be hired, an office rota set up, a bank account opened, possible routes investigated. It was also decided that no contact should be made with the police until plans were further consolidated.

That same day Butler faxed Sir Michael Richardson a fuller account of their scheme. The aim of the marches (this said) was to support the rally due to be held in Hyde Park on 10 July, and 'make clear to politicians that there is a huge and significant strength of feeling in the countryside.' No one could tell how many people might take part, but it was important 'that a proportion, even if small, of those involved walk the complete route.' As for public relations – good coverage in the press, on radio and television would be essential, but the timing of press releases would need 'careful consideration', so that the story did not blow itself out prematurely. Attached to the memorandum was a preliminary budget which estimated that the organisational costs would amount to between £9,000 and £12,000.

So, over a kitchen table top, a mighty enterprise was launched. Even a modest office was going to need finance, and the most urgent problem was fund-raising. Miller Mundy had already obtained a promise of support from the Campaign for Hunting (an arm of the BFSS), but said he would prefer to raise money privately, if he could, as he wanted his initiative to embrace all forms of rural sports and activities, rather than be confined to hunting alone.

After a third meeting, attended by fifteen people, he began his search for funds by ringing up shooting friends. The response was 'quite extraordinary.' One after another people wrote cheques.

Each listened to him for about ten minutes, and the only question ever asked was 'How much do you want?' Soon he had cheques for £100, £250, £500, then two for £2,500 and one for £5,000. In a few days he had amassed £12,500.

In the minds of the organisers march-routes were rapidly taking shape. For Miller Mundy, the symbolic start-point must be the village of Caldbeck, in the Lakes, where the legendary huntsman John Peel lies buried. The first march would set off from there. A second would depart from Coldstream, on the border between Scotland and England, and would unite with the Lakeland column on its way south. A third march would leave Machynlleth, in West Wales, with a subsidiary column perhaps coming across the heads of the South Wales mining valleys to join it. Finally, a West Country march would start from Madron, near Land's End, and advance across the southern counties of England. The aim was to recruit the maximum possible number of core marchers – those who would complete the whole route to London – and to swell the columns with day-walkers, who would join in for shorter stretches. The core marchers would be fed and housed at the end of each leg, but others would have to fend for themselves.

The next step was to sound out key men in the field. Together with Sam Butler, Miller Mundy drove out to Llandinam, in Powys, to meet David Jones and his wife Sue in the little white huntsman's cottage across the lane from the David Davies kennels. When they arrived in the afternoon, there was nobody else present, but the call had gone out into the valleys and mountains: at about 4 pm cars began to draw up, and soon a dozen men had packed into the small dining room for a magnificent tea of sandwiches, cakes, scones and flapjacks. Some were still in their hunting clothes and had been up since 5 am, out on emergency calls from farmers who had lost lambs to foxes.

As they heard Miller Mundy lay out his ideas, they gave no immediate effusive reaction; but the atmosphere was electric with interest, and the listeners, with their sharp eyes watching every move, reminded Butler of a pack of terriers on the alert for rats. Suddenly, as they saw the point, they gained confidence, began to ask questions, and agreed that, yes, support would be forthcoming in Wales.

13

Miller Mundy's next target was the north. He and Charles Mann drove up to the Scotch Corner Hotel, where a meeting of key personnel had been arranged by Frank Houghton-Brown, Joint Master of the Middleton Hunt. Very tall and slim, dark, good-looking and barely into his thirties, Houghton-Brown had become a terrier man on leaving school, and his deceptively quiet manner masked absolute dedication to his sport. He had assembled all the best people from his country, and once again the seeds of the plan fell into fertile ground: the meeting was enthusiastic, and promises of support were immediately forthcoming.

As the travellers left, someone asked them where they were going, and when they said, 'The Lake District', dire predictions followed about the difficulty they would have in getting the fell boys up and doing. In some apprehension they drove on into the Lakes, stayed the night with a friend, and next day headed for their rendezvous at the Salutation Inn in the village of Threlkeld. On the way they visited Barry Todhunter, huntsmen of the Blencathra Hounds (John Peel's pack), and went on to reconnoitre their projected start-point, the churchyard at Caldbeck. Then, because they had time in hand, they decided to go for a walk up the fell; but Miller Mundy was so tired that after a while he lay on the grass and fell asleep. Mann climbed on to the top of a hill and sat there for a while rehearsing the speech he was about to give, then came back down to collect his colleague.

At the inn the upstairs snooker room filled with powerful-looking men. It was not often that representatives of all the fell packs met harmoniously, and their presence was due to the unemphatic authority of Edmund Porter, who, by skilful leader-ship over the past decade, had done much to bring them together. It was he who had called the meeting, and he who now chaired it. At first things did not go quite as the team from Gloucestershire had hoped, for the floor was held by Sandy Foster, local representative of the BFSS, who talked for nearly an hour with immense enthusiasm about the Hyde Park rally and arrangements for travelling to London. Mann feared he had lost the initiative, and when Miller Mundy at last got a chance to air his vision of the marches, the audience remained silent. But then Mann spoke, and afterwards when Miller Mundy asked, 'Any support from you boys?' a Cumbrian voice said, 'I think we ought to get behind it.' There was a stir in the room, and John Harrison, Huntsman of the Ullswater Fell Hounds, offered to walk to London there and then. When Miller Mundy brought up the question of compensation for loss of wages for anyone who gave up his time, a discussion broke out about how people could be sponsored with locally-raised funds.

There could be no doubt that the march was on, and immediately it was clear that Harrison – a tall, well-built man in his thirties – would become a key figure in it. With pints of beer coming up in relays from below, the meeting went on to discuss the route. Mann's original plan was that from Caldbeck the Lakeland column should head due east, to join the Scottish marchers as soon as possible; but this idea did not go down well. As one, the fell huntsmen were determined that the march should go though all their own countries – and so, path by path, lane by lane, hill by hill, the delegates hammered out a new and more tortuous route which would join the northern march at Northallerton.

Having started at six, the meeting ended at 9.30 pm. Mann immediately drove south, dropping Miller Mundy home at 1.30 am, and reaching base an hour later. Both, though exhausted, were in a state of euphoria.

The final provincial meeting took place in Devon in a 15th-century country house near Okehampton, where a friend had offered David Latham the use of a large room. For this excursion to the West Country Miller Mundy was accompanied by Chipps Mann and Luke Annaly (Lord Annaly), who had been brought in to help with the organisation. Chipps sensed a spooky atmosphere in the huge, square house built round a central courtyard: certainly it was freezing cold in the baronial chamber, and she fervently wished that someone would set off a blaze in the big open fireplace.

Never mind the discomfort, she decided. Latham had been extremely efficient. Not only had he collected nearly thirty key people: he was already one step ahead, with maps on the table and a route planned in his mind. Miller Mundy had hardly outlined his idea before the route was being discussed: the Cornish march was practically in being. As he was leaving, their host, the owner of the house, came up to him and said, 'The last time we had a meeting like this here was during the Civil War.' The hair on Miller Mundy's neck crawled, for he realised that the mood of country people was not much different from that of 350 years earlier. As he put it, 'They wanted to stand up and do something, rather than just keep reacting.' Always a worrier, he was already nervous about the scale of the reaction which his scheme was eliciting: he had hardly expected people to respond with such passion.

On Monday 14 April the Manns opened an office in a pigsty converted into a workshop; the room – with a low ceiling, walls roughly painted white, and a French window opening on to a gravel sweep – had been used by a girl who restored watercolours, but luckily she had just moved out. The single telephone point was augmented by three more lines, a photocopier hired, some old furniture brought from Sam Butler's office in Burford, and Chipps's computer moved out of the house. The marches office was up and running: its great merit was always that it could and did react quickly. The staff might be amateurs, but they were never hampered by bureaucratic restrictions, and took decisions immediately.

There was a tremendous amount of planning to be done – and almost all of it was breaking new ground, for none of the people involved had ever tackled a project of this kind. First, they had to carve each route into daily stretches of eighteen or twenty miles. Then they had to work out precise arrangements for every day: times and places for morning-starts, mid-morning refreshments, lunch-halts, tea-breaks. In dozens of different areas they had to unearth coordinators – local people who would find enough volunteers to pick up the core marchers in the evenings, give them baths, supper, bed and breakfast, and return them to the start-point next morning.

Detailed breakdowns resolved that the northern marches would take twenty-four days (including rest days), the Cornish march seventeen and the Welsh fourteen. All would finish in the outskirts of London on 9 July, so that the marchers could be taken into Hyde Park by bus for the rally next day. Working backwards from that date, the organisers set their starts as 14 June from Caldbeck, 15 June from Coldstream, 22 June from Madron, and 27 June from Machynlleth and St. Clears. One early decision was that there

16

should be a total ban on animals: clearly, many of those taking part would be tempted to turn out on horseback, or bring dogs with them – but the presence of four-footed creatures, it was decided, would create intolerable risks on public roads.

One area in which the organisers needed expert guidance was liaison with the police. At first they had no idea how or where to begin; then, luckily, they made contact with George Walker, a retired Superintendent living in Gloucestershire, who gave them excellent advice. Of course they must work within the Public Order Act, he told them, and use common sense. But there was no reason to be nervous of the police. 'They can't stop you,' he said, 'so work with them on a professional basis. Tell them what you're doing, and you'll get all the cooperation you need.' This they decided to do, when the time seemed ripe.

The central organisation was carried out from the farm office, where the volunteers had the formidable task of photocopying 1:50,000 Ordnance Survey maps and pasting sheets together to cover each day's route. This operation took up so much space that some of the team had to move out into the barbecue space at the end of the swimming pool, next door, where they teetered dangerously back and forth round the edge of the water.

But the bulk of detailed planning was delegated to the hunts through whose countries the marchers would pass – and the response was magnificent. As Mann put it, 'We were amazed by the reaction we got. People on the ground were longing to contribute, and to provide beds or meals or coffee-breaks was a way of taking an active part.' In the West Country, David Latham and his wife Jo did an immense amount themselves, not only reconnoitring the entire route, but also finding core walkers and coordinators.

When not working in the office, Mann, Butler and Annaly drove all over the country meeting bunches of coordinators and recruiting more core walkers. Coordinators were asked to study each day's route in detail, 'taking into account local knowledge and land-owners, footpaths, bridlepaths and possible alternative routes.' They were also requested to 'spread the word and encourage day-walkers by the thousand!' Their particular targets should include gamekeepers, beaters, cartridge manufacturers, clay-pigeon shooters,

17

fishermen, blacksmiths, saddlers, vets, feed merchants, pony-club organisers, Young Farmers' Club secretaries, foresters and gardeners. If possible, they should arrange to place leaflets in pubs two days ahead of the marchers 'to alert people to what is happening', and have welcoming posters put up in fields along the route.

On 20 May, with all the routes fully worked out, Butler wrote to the police forces in every region through which the marchers would pass, predicting that each column might be as many as 200 strong on any one day. Replies were helpful, but far from enthusiastic. To a man the police chiefs said that they could not condone what the organisers were planning, and, for the safety of walkers and other road users, advised them not to go through with their scheme. Undeterred, Butler prepared detailed operational orders for every marching day, and between 6 and 10 June sent them out to the police contacts he had already established, giving routes, timings and relevant telephone numbers. (These, it turned out, went down extremely well: after the event, the police commended the organisers, saying they had never had such a presentation put before them).

As interest built up, entries in the marches office Message Book became steadily more hectic: 'Tom Yates, v.g. old hairy trade unionist, used to hunt with Heythrop, voice for PR . . . John Francome will come to any photocall . . . John Oaksey will drop July cup to support rally . . . Cleveland Police Area Six needs to be notified as you are going thro' Sedgefield etc. . . . LOO PAPER AND LIGHT BULB . . . Ed Tate getting more fluorescent vests . . . What has happened to NFU? . . . David Maclean, MP for Penrith and Border, will be at Caldbeck start . . . Gamekeepers are good news . . . Celebrities – Who will be there? Get minder for each . . Sir David Allingham from King's Lynn: he cannot help with the marches, but is sending a cheque as a donation, to buy beer for the marchers. . . Please tell Amanda contact re Dame Kiri Te Kanawa . . . Stephen Hill does NOT need a bed in this area, as he lives here . . . URGENT – sign forms for three mobile phones, all direct debits.'

Another area in which the organisers knew they were weak was that of public relations. The whole point of the marches was that they should constitute a major public-relations exercise, putting over the country point of view; and yet nobody knew how best to tackle the media. In contrast with the BFSS, who had spokesmen deployed all over the country, already touting the rally, the march office had no press officer and no experience of media relations. Miller Mundy was anxious that news of the initiative should not leak out prematurely: he was afraid that if this happened, public interest might die long before the marches reached London. He was also nervous that marchers would talk to the press out of turn – that some aristocratic hunting person, unburdened by brains, might undermine the whole initiative by braying inanities. Early instructions therefore forbade individual walkers to speak to the press, and all the organisation was done under cover, with an embargo set for 12 June.

The organising team became determined to find a professional public relations officer, but the task proved harder than expected, and by Monday, 2 June, feeling they had reached a crisis, they set themselves an ultimatum: if they had not recruited someone by the next Friday, they would have to take on the job themselves. Contigency plans were put in hand to set up a press office in a Portakabin staffed by Chipps, Amanda Butler and other volunteers taken out of the main office.

Then on Wednesday 4 June, two days before the deadline, they at last discovered the person they were looking for in the form of Amanda Courtney, a six-foot blonde with her own public-relations business, Courtlake Marketing, in the Cotswold village of Northleach. A professional to her finger-tips, Amanda proved as formidably effective as her appearance was striking: contributing her services for no fee – the refund of expenses only – she plunged into action to lay the foundations of a nation-wide media campaign.

At first there was some tension between her and Janet George, press officer of the BFSS, another powerful operator with long experience in the game. For a couple of days it seemed that one irresistible force had run headlong into another, since at that stage the BFSS were already actively promoting their rally, while the march organisers were trying to keep their preparations under wraps. Contradictory rumours proliferated: that the BFSS wanted to dissociate themselves from the marches, that they were trying to take over the marches, that the marches would undermine the rally

. . . But the conflict was soon resolved, and all parties pressed ahead with their plans.

Throughout the preparations everyone was keenly aware of the risks involved: that marchers would be knocked down by cars or lorries, or that antis would try to block their advance. Chipps Mann, in particular, became apprehensive, waking up at night 'convinced either that someone would be killed on the road, or that we'd have some monumental punch-up.' Sam Butler never thought there would be fights, but he was worried about the safety of all the men and women marching on main roads, and after obtaining several quotations, he took out took out third-party, public liability insurance. For a premium of £1,450, he obtained £2 million of cover for the period of 12 June to 10 July. The office, unable to insure individual walkers, for financial reasons, strongly advised everyone to take out insurance of their own.

One key figure, not directly attached to the office, but working in the wings, was John Fretwell, burly huntsman of the Stowe School beagles, who in April launched the Union of Country Sports Workers and rapidly acquired more than a thousand members. Since the aim of this 'trade association' was to 'be an effective voice speaking for those who stand to lose most if country sports are made illegal,' Fretwell was a natural ally for the march organisers, and agreed to help with publicity when news of the enterprise broke.

As the start of the marches drew closer, momentum built up in the office. In all, some twenty volunteers were recruited: two were on duty at any one time, the place was open – at first – during normal business hours. Then, as the pressure increased, work began at 7.30 am and was often still going on at 9.30 pm, 'well into second whisky time.' The volume of telephone, fax and postal traffic became phenomenal: altogether, 30,000 sheets of A4 paper were used. For a major corporation, that might have been a single mail-shot; but for a bunch of amateurs working in a converted pig-sty, it was no mean output. The spirit of the enterprise was epitomised by Lindy Allen, a schoolteacher living nearby: wishing to contribute to the effort, but unable to work in the office because of her job, she hit on the idea of making, and bringing in, lunch for the staff two days a week.

Between 6 and 10 June an operational order for every day's march, together with a copy of the 1:50,000 map showing the route, went out to the police contacts already made. The organisers predicted that on each march between 100 and 200 people would be walking every day, and they enclosed their thoughts on support vehicles, communications (mobile phones and radios), the problem of whether people should walk on the left or the right of the road, and above all safety, both of the walkers and of other road-users. The response was extraordinarily positive, and in the whole country only two modifications of routes were needed, one to avoid an accident black-spot in Yorkshire.

The leader of each march would appoint stewards, to act for a day at a time, and briefing notes for these marshals echoed the nervousness of the organisers:

* Please at all times keep your eyes peeled for trouble. If anyone is seen to be stirring things up or is the worse for alcohol, they must be sent home.
* No animals allowed on the march whatsoever, whatever the reason (except guide-dogs, of course.)
* Please familiarize yourself with the Highway Code.
* Report any damage. Close all gates. No litter.

A Code of Conduct, issued to all core walkers, emphasised that 'safety and decent behaviour must be paramount at all times.' Adverse publicity, said the leaflet, 'will jeopardise the whole march. All walkers must behave in a dignified and orderly manner – and whatever the provocation, there must be no retaliation, because we are ambassadors for the countryside.'

CHAPTER THREE

Googlies in the Park

While the marches took shape, Simon Clarke and his colleagues at the BFSS were moving forward in fits and starts as they planned the Hyde Park rally.* The insistent desire of the Society's members was to march on Downing Street or the House of Commons *en masse;* and because this was impossible, ways of stopping them had to be devised. One early plan was that a mounted delegation should ride to Westminster, past Buckingham Palace, like the Household Cavalry, with plenty of horses, tractors, trailers and other farm machinery, while the assembled throng remained in the park and watched its progress on a giant television screen. Presently this idea was abandoned in favour of a straightforward rally on the flat area in the north-east corner of the park known as the Cavalry Parade Ground, once the home of the famous Reformer's Tree, but now only of its successor, a lamp-post bearing that name. A delegation would still carry a petition to Downing Street, but it would be a small group, and it would travel by bus.

The organisers' greatest difficulty lay in trying to understand the regulations that control public behaviour in Hyde Park. Dating from the reign of Charles II, who was displeased by the number of citizens using his parks, the rules were originally designed to deny access to as many people as possible, and to this day they remain thoroughly confusing. One problem is that they are frequently amended; another that their interpretation seems to vary according

---

* On 26 March the BFSS announced that it was joining forces with two relatively new bodies, the Countryside Movement and the Countryside Business Group, under the umbrella title The Countryside Alliance. In this narrative, for the sake of clarity, the Society's more familiar name and initials have been retained.

to the day of the week, the phases of the moon or the nature of the festivity being planned.

Hanbury-Tenison and Clarke had '*the* most frightful difficulties with the Royal Parks Agency,' because they did not know how to deal with this unique body. Agency officials told them that the Royal Parks Police Force – a separate entity – had grave objections to the idea of a mid-week rally, but that the decision as to whether or not it could be held rested with the Heritage Minister, Virginia Bottomley. Then, as soon as the General Election was called for 1 May, they told Mrs Bottomley that it would be inappropriate for her to take any decision, and the matter was put on hold.

In Clarke's view, 'The fact was that they weren't really entitled to object. The Reformer's Tree is a traditional meeting-place and rally-point, and, provided we could prove we were a respectable organisation, they hadn't many rights to stop us.'

In an attempt to clarify matters, Peter Voute, Executive Director of the BFSS, sought the advice of Alan Evershed, a retired Chief Superintendent who had served for thirty years in the Metropolitan Police and still had many contacts in the force. Although an out-and-out townie, who claimed not to understand country people (even though he 'once went for a whole weekend to Norfolk'), Evershed proved thoroughly helpful. Through him, the organisers were at least able to gain a better idea of the way minds were working, both in the Met. and in the Royal Parks Police.

One weekend, while Clarke was at home in Dorset, 'an amazing thing happened.' Along came 'an eccentric photographer called Mark Miller Mundy,' who was visiting his sister-in-law nearby, and expounded his embryonic plan for the marches. Clarke thought it sounded a good idea, even if he was not sure how much of a stir it would create. He too was anxious that the protest movement should be widened beyond field sports, to embrace all country activities; so when he had writing paper printed specifically for the event, he headed it THE COUNTRYSIDE RALLY, *11 AM THURSDAY 10TH JULY IN HYDE PARK,* and although he gave the address and telephone number of the BFSS, he deliberately left off the Society's name.

Political developments lent his deliberations ever-increasing urgency. First there was Labour's landslide victory in the General

Election of 1 May. Next came the announcement on 22 May that Michael Foster, Labour Member of Parliament for Worcester, and the House of Commons's most active opponent of hunting, had come top in the ballot for Private Members' Bills. Then on 16 June Foster announced at a news conference that he would table his Wild Mammals (Hunting with Dogs) Bill in the Commons next day, and the Bill received its first reading on the 17th. The need for a big and successful demonstration of feeling became greater by the week.

There was, however, one major problem. Was the gathering to be a rally or an event? The difference was crucial, because in Hyde Park a rally can be held free, but for an event the organisers have to pay – and in this instance it looked as if the fee could be between £100,000 and £200,000. What *is* the difference? 'You ask me,' said Clarke, after months of argument. 'The rules are woolly. You can speak at a rally, but you can't have too much entertainment. At an event you can have whatever you like – Pavarotti, for instance. But then you have to fence in a perimeter, and make an enclosure.'

Meetings with David Welch, the parks' Chief Executive, were friendly enough, but failed to break the deadlock. An excellent gardener – author of a book on roses – and a well-known after-dinner speaker with a good sense of humour, but not a country-man, Welch wove his mysteries so skilfully that the BFSS never quite knew where they were. In cricketing terms, he was the Shane Warne of Hyde Park: was he bowling leg breaks, googlies, flippers, or what? The field sports team never quite managed to read his hand. Time and again they played and missed. At one stage, for instance, Welch said that he had the Gay Pride rally booked for the weekend before July 10, and another immediately afterwards, and 'did not want a precedent.' Which way was that one meant to spin? When Clarke murmured that he thought it slightly unfair to compare the Countryside Rally with Gay Pride, Welch answered, 'I suppose that's fair comment. I consider you people mainstream meat-eaters.'

Among the carnivores, no one had a more frustrating time than Andrew Sallis, a 24-year-old composer and teacher who had got a First in music at Manchester University and had then done postgraduate work at Cambridge, where he hunted the Trinity

College beagles. In March he had been appointed Composer in Residence at Charterhouse School for the following academic year; this meant that he had the summer free, and, being addicted to hunting, he offered his services 'as stamp-licker/ dog's-body' to the BFSS, who promptly signed him on as Entertainment Co-ordinator.

When he arrived in Kennington at the end of April, negotiations were already in progress with two musical groups: the Polypipe Rossington Brass Band, and the chorus of 'Jorrocks,' the musical staged at Stowe School in February, to great acclaim, by members of the Bicester with Whaddon Chase Hunt. Over the next few weeks he reinforced these early recruits by booking a splendid variety of acts: ten fell singers, a jazz band from the Royal Academy of Music, Jackie Allen and the Milestones, a constantly-fluctuating number of French horns (from fifteen to sixty), a barber's shop choir, and Scottish pipers with a specially-composed 'Macnab's Reveille'.

In due course his role was extended, and he became the deviser of the entire rally programme. Other staff at the BFSS worked out which of the numerous invited celebrities should speak, and for how long, but it was Sallis's job to interleave the speeches – each scheduled to last between ninety seconds and six minutes – with the items of entertainment. Alas, the restrictions demanded by the Parks Agency played havoc with his plans, which he had to change with bewildering frequency. As he put it, 'the to-ing and fro-ing of ideas for speakers and acts was incredible.' In the two months preceding 10 July his rally order went through over thirty drafts, which were 'circulated, analysed and systematically destroyed.'

Various off-stage ideas came and went. One was that there should be a mass-release of 15,000 balloons, each with the name of a living hound on it. The organisers had not realised that to loose off balloons they would need a licence from the Civil Air Authority, because the park is under the Heathrow flight-path – so the plan was scrapped. (An echo of it survived in the flotilla of large, white, tethered balloons bearing the names of counties, which acted as excellent rallying points). One day in March Clarke happened to meet Major Edward Camilleri, General Manager of the Royal Pigeon Racing Association, who considered that under a Labour government his sport was the sixth most threatened pastime, and asked if the rally could include a release of pigeons – which, in the end, it did.

Advertising for the rally was launched at Badminton on 9 May. The first posters were displayed, and lapel-stickers became very much the vogue during the three-day event.

Immediately after that, the BFSS fortuitously gained another invaluable young recruit. Rosalie Coutts, always known as Posy, was then twenty-seven and had served four-and-a-half years in the army, finishing as a captain in the Royal Logistic Corps, the adjutant of her battalion in Bosnia. Having left the army in June 1996, she travelled and worked on cattle stations in Australia, New Zealand and Argentina before returning to England at the beginning of May 1997. Back in London, she heard about the rally and telephoned her friend Camilla Charteris, Robin Hanbury-Tenison's personal assistant, to see if any jobs were going. Camilla told her that the place was fizzing with activity, and suggested she send in her *curriculum vitae*.

The BFSS had belatedly realised that they needed somebody to take charge of transport, and, partly because almost all Posy's military experience had been in that field, she got the job. Arriving at the office in Kennington on 12 May, she was 'staggered to find how vague the organisation was.' At that stage it was hoped that the rally would attract 20,000 people, but nobody had made any arrangements for bringing them into London. When Posy asked for the file on transport, she was told that none existed, and she could hardly believe that the event was scheduled for July 1997. Were people really talking about July 1998?

The only way she could evolve a plan was by finding out what was happening. She therefore initiated a letter and proforma, asking about travel plans. The documents went out to 4,000 people – all masters of fox-hounds, stag-hounds and beagles, associated sporting organisations, tradesmen, the racing world – and every recipient was asked to duplicate the documents and send copies to members.

People began ringing up by the dozen to say that they were organising group transport; but it quickly became clear that they were all expecting to drive into Hyde Park and leave their coaches there. This, Posy told them, was simply not feasible: numbers were already too great. At the most Hyde Park could take 140 buses, at a charge of £100 apiece. Research had shown that 52 able-bodied people take about seven minutes to leave a coach, less mobile passengers about nine. The equation was impossible. The park would not be able to cope with the influx predicted.

When the first wave of proformas came back, it suggested that about 250 buses might head for London. Soon the number was up to 300. With an average of just over fifty seats per coach, this alone meant a crowd of over 15,000, all pouring in at much the same time. Seeing the scale of the problem, Posy went to the Coach Advisory Service of the Metropolitan Police, at the headquarters on the Embankment. There again she was dumbfounded. Supposing the Service must have some plan for the rally, she found it had none. Rallies usually took place at weekends, someone told her. The Service had never had to deal with so large a number of people coming into town on a weekday.

Posy realised that it would be impossible for coaches to ferry such a horde right into Hyde Park without bringing London to a halt – and if that happened, many supporters would themselves be stuck in traffic jams. The answer, she saw, was to identify outlying parking-space on which buses could set their passengers down. Aiming to find places at all points of the compass, which could take traffic from north, south, east and west, she eventually secured nine, the biggest Wembley Stadium, with room for 350 coaches, the next largest Battersea, with 200 spaces. One disappointment was Syon Park, which would have taken 160, but could not in the end be used, because the company due to run a shuttle service into town let the organisers down.

At the BFSS people were wildly excited by the way the numbers kept rocketing up; yet each morning, as she came into the office, Posy half-hoped that they would level off. They never did. By the end of June the total of incoming coaches had passed 800, and as she had room for only 820, she had to bring in Earl's Court, which could take another hundred.

It was clear that many of the prospective passengers had never been to London: coach firms kept ringing in, worried that their people might be so bewildered by the size and complexity of the capital that they would never find their way to Hyde Park. Posy therefore put together an operational instruction which included every detail of how to move from set-down point to final destination. She also laid on more than 100 marshals, to meet buses as they arrived, and hand out the instruction, along with a map, a song-sheet and free Underground tickets, to every passenger. Other marshals would meet the special trains: people arriving at Paddington could easily walk down to the park, but those coming in to Euston or King's Cross also received guidance and free tube tickets. In tube stations yet more marshals were on hand to direct rally-bound travellers on to the correct platforms and escalators.

One of her main worries was that antis might try to close Underground stations by means of bomb warnings. To minimise this risk, together with Peter Voute she liaised with the Metropolitan Police and had several meetings with London Transport's Underground Emergency Planner, who showed her round the Emergency Control Room. Throughout her negotiations she found London Transport 'incredibly helpful', not least over the sale of tickets: they let her buy £75,000 worth 'at a very good price,' and on sale or return. She also visited the control rooms on the Docklands Light Railway, which would be bringing people in from the seventy coaches booked into the Docklands park.

At BFSS headquarters people were working at higher and higher pressure. More staff had been taken on to cope with the extra work-load. A hot-line had been set up, and the long, elegant board-room converted into an Operations Room, with Peter Voute, the Society's Executive Director, in charge. Nevertheless, misunderstandings continued to proliferate. On 22 May the Society obtained the signature of the new Secretary of State for Heritage, Chris Smith, and assumed this meant that the rally could go ahead. But, Clarke found, 'we soon discovered that nothing meant what it said,' and towards the end of May he decided that the Society needed professional help. As he put it, 'We were getting out of our depth.'

To cut through the confusion, they sought the advice of Major Michael Parker, an outstanding entrepreneur and organiser who, from a tiny basement flat in Earl's Court, had laid on numerous major public events. Not only had he master-minded the Royal

Tournament for many years, and in 1995 produced the VE and VJ Day celebrations; almost more important, he was used, from long experience, to dealing with the Royal Parks Agency. Extra work was hardly what he wanted at that moment, since he was at full stretch preparing for the Pageant of the Horse, an immense event featuring 1,000 horses, due to take place at Windsor on 7 July, three days before the rally. Nevertheless, he agreed to help, and met the organisers in the park on 27 May.

Having talked through their plans, and heard how negotiations were going round in circles, he decided that although the BFSS was working on the right lines, everything needed pulling together. Because it was clear that numbers would far exceed the original estimate of 20,000, he told the organisers that they must come clean with the Parks Agency about the likely total: they must give a realistic estimate, and make realistic arrangements.

Further, he foresaw (and told the Parks representatives and police) that the people coming in from all over the country would be a very unusual mix, quite unlike a normal London crowd. They would not want to go shopping or sight-seeing: they would come for the rally alone. Moreover, many of them might arrive early. All this meant that 'to keep them contented and well-disciplined, we would need to entertain them.' For this purpose he proposed that, apart from the speeches and acts on the main stage, there should be seven smaller, satellite stages, from which 'wandering minstrels' – singers, guitar-players, pipers, sword-dancers – could play to sections of the crowd. The satellite units would be needed anyway as relay stations for the sound-amplification system, and they would make good focal points.

After a meeting with David Welch on 8 June, he thought that all this had been agreed. 'But then suddenly it *wasn't* agreed. We could have the satellite stages, but we couldn't have anybody on them. We couldn't have people playing music. Certainly no music could be amplified. The parks people said that if we had entertainment and singing, the rally would become an event, and they would charge us rent.'

With these circular arguments unresolved, Parker 'sat in the middle and tried to massage everything forward.' But he was adamant that the provision of facilities – lavatories, crash barriers, first aid, security, fire cover, sound systems – must be put into professional hands, and he brought in Unusual Services and Pacesetter, the companies which do all the production management for his major events. These firms immediately took over all practical arrangements, organising contractors and bringing in Showsec Security to provide a full security service on the day. With numbers constantly moving upwards, the new management aimed high and provided facilities for 100,000 people.

Parker contributed his personal services free, and everyone agreed that he brought off a phenomenal feat of diplomacy or liaison or massage – whatever term best described his role. In Simon Clarke's view, 'Everything changed when we got him involved, and when he brought his amazing skills to bear.' Parker's recommendations quadrupled the BFSS's budget, which leapt from £25,000 to £100,000 overnight (in the end it was over £300,000); but he selflessly gave his own time during a period of extreme pressure, and it was cruel indeed that persistent deluges forced him at the last minute to cancel the Pageant of the Horse, on which he had worked for two years.

Posy the blonde Transport Goddess, equally, worked wonders with her bus-parks and stewards, her liaison with police and tube operators; and if the rally had one unsung hero, it was Peter Voute, who, in the final hectic period, brought all his previous military experience to bear, working immensely long days, and devoting all his time to the project.

Yet at BFSS headquarters the situation remained fraught, and for Clarke the final three weeks before 10 July were 'a hair-raising time.' Still lacking definite permission, but not daring to admit it, and faced with having to entertain a crowd of at least 50,000, the organisers decided to press ahead regardless: they knew that, in an extremity, they could go to the park without a licence or public-address system, and hold *some* sort of rally, even if it ended in disappointment or fiasco.

All through their preparations they were dogged by fear that antis might infiltrate the crowd and try to take over the stand. In March, after the Grand National had been suddenly cancelled in response to a bomb-threat, it was put about that the telephone warnings had been made by the IRA. Some people, however, believed that the disruption was the work of the Animal Liberation Front – and no one could be sure that animal-rights fanatics would not try to spoil the party in Hyde Park.

CHAPTER FOUR

Down from the North

The official starting place of the marches was Caldbeck; but by the middle of June the tide of enthusiasm was running so strongly in the north that Scottish farmers and hunting people set up a preliminary support march of their own, and at 8 am on 13 June a group set out from Kettleholm, south of Lockerbie, to walk from there via Gretna Green to Carlisle, a distance of over twenty miles. That same day the Manns, the Miller Mundys, Amanda Courtney and others travelled up to Carlisle for the first briefing of core walkers, held in the Cumbrian Hotel, a few yards from the railway station.

This gathering made it immediately clear that the prospective marchers were a world away from the purple-faced toffs whom antis love to hate. These were hard fell men, with close-cropped heads and blunt northern accents, wearing T-shirts and jeans, and they listened carefully as Charles Mann confirmed their routine for the next three-and-a-half weeks. They would be driven to the start each morning, he told them: support vehicles would carry first-aid kit, drinks, sleeping bags and pillows in case anyone passed out. Placards would be provided for selected marchers to carry, along with leaflets for distribution to spectators and passers-by. Mobile telephones and CB radios would keep the front and back of the column in touch with each other, and with the support vehicles – but be warned: mobile phones do not work in much of the Lake District. Only if the user is on top of a fell are they effective.

Having appointed various individuals to carry out particular tasks – acting as marshals, dealing with the media – he emphasised the need for decorum. 'We have got to get from here to London without any incidents,' he said. 'Whatever happens, we don't want a punch-up. The march is a massive, peaceful protest. If this one doesn't work, the next may be rather different. But this one is peaceful. If we find antis staging a sit-down in the road, we do not try to walk through them. We do not trample over them. We stop, call the police on the mobile and wait for them to clear the way.'

With that he handed out the core walkers' bright lemon- yellow T-shirts, with slogans in black fore and aft: THE VOICE OF THE COUNTRYSIDE and LISTEN TO US. 'Wear them one way one day, the other the next,' he instructed. As the meeting came to an end, people were gathering in the market square, for Peter Wybergh, Master of the Cumberland Farmers' Hunt, had determined that his people, also, should play a part in this historic event. At five o'clock they joined forces with some of the men from Kettleholm, and strode off through Carlisle to walk the thirteen miles to Caldbeck.

There, in the hamlet of stone houses cradled by fells, the Manns had booked in for the night at the pub, the Oddfellows Arms, where, in the bar, there hangs the only known portrait of John Woodcock Graves, who wrote the words of the song 'D'ye Ken John Peel?' At about 7pm, together with a friend, Charles set out on foot in the general direction of Carlisle and walked five miles down the River Caldew to meet his approaching army. By the time they all came in, around 9.30, the men from Kettleholm had covered thirty-five miles on foot that day. Local people had been drifting into Caldbeck all evening, and suddenly the pub was swamped by a seething mass of farmers, all goaded by a powerful thirst. When the bar closed at 11pm, hunting songs were roaring out with a volume that threatened the windows.

The morning of 14 June was grey and dreary. Clouds lowered on the fells all round, blotting out the tops; roofs and roads glistened in the drizzle. But Caldbeck was buzzing from 6 am, because rumours of major action by antis had brought out the police in force. The threat never materialised – only half a dozen seedy-looking protesters turned out – but by 8.30 there were at least 400 people crowding into and around the long, flat graveyard to witness the send-off ceremony.

The focus of attention was the grave of John Peel, who died in 1854 at the age of seventy-eight. Among the VIPs waiting in front of his tall, whitewashed gravestone was David Maclean, the local Member of Parliament, who had come to support the enterprise. As he waited, he spoke with feeling of the 1992 Earth Summit at Rio, in which he had taken part as a Government Minister. One of the key principles formulated there was that indigenous communities play a vital role in sustainable development, and that their identities, culture and traditions should therefore be protected. In Rio, he agreed, people had been talking principally about primitive minorities such as the tree-dwellers of Sarawak. 'But,' he said, 'it seems to me that exactly the same principles apply in Cumbria. Here we have an indigenous people, with its own culture and heritage, and it is surely the Government's duty to protect rather than destroy it.'

As 9 am approached, the Rector of Caldbeck, the Reverend Ron Johns, spoke a few words to wish the marchers a safe journey, and Barry Todhunter, in his red hunting coat and black cap, sent shivers up many a spine with two thin, raucous blasts on a replica of John Peel's little bugle-shaped horn. With that, he and John Harrison led out of the churchyard, past the posse of antis screaming their ritual abuse, past a sturdy gamekeeper with a placard announcing THE LAST MAN TO BAN HUNTING WAS HITLER, and away up a lane that led to the open fells.

So began the peasants' revolt of 1997 – and the first morning of the first march was enough to reveal how deeply this new protest was rooted in the earth. Several of the ten core walkers were hunting men and women, it is true, but others were not, and among the hundred-odd followers who joined them for the day there were foresters and doctors, rabbit-catchers and lawyers, gamekeepers, water-bailiffs, gardeners and school-masters.

Leading the pack was Barry Todhunter, a small, spare man whose spectacles gave him a studious appearance – more of an academic than a fell-man. Yet there was nothing academic about the pace he set. Desribing it as 'a gentle stroll', he went off at a rate that quickly strung the column out over hundreds of yards. Soon he had reached the house in which he was born and, on the other side of the lane, the home of the mountaineer Chris Bonington. There he and John Harrison changed out of their heavy hunting coats into lighter, more informal gear and left the road altogether, striking up into the grass and heather of the high fells.

Like many of those with him, Todhunter stood to lose his entire livelihood if hunting with hounds were banned. No matter that he had worked as a hunt servant for twenty-six years. Everything would go: 'Number one, my job. Number two, my house. Number three, my vehicle.' That was his reason for walking – but not for walking so fast: he knew that on the first day the party had a long way to go, and he wanted to reach the evening rendezvous in good time.

It was fitting that he should lead the first day, for the route ran through the Blencathra country, of which he knew every how and dale, every dod and ghyll, every pike and rigg and cove. Commitments at the kennels had prevented him from signing on as a core walker; but the tall, long-striding John Harrison was definitely going all the way to London. Ever since 1984 he had been away from his home country, working as a hunt servant, and for the past five seasons he had hunted the Toronto and North York hounds in Canada. From a distance, during his absence abroad, he had watched with dismay as anti-hunting pressure built up in Britain, feeling helpless at his inability to contribute to the debate. Now, on the march to Hyde Park, he had his chance. As he left the churchyard at Caldbeck, 'not really knowing what lay ahead,' he was very much aware that he carried 'the hopes and wishes of our Lakeland sportsmen and women' with him, and he was determined to do his best.

Out for the day was Monty Farish, a genial, heavyweight mole-catcher whose work gave him access to 40,000 acres of farmland. Describing the weather as 'gair rowky' (real misty), he recalled how, as a schoolboy, he would skin his victims on the move between one set of traps and the next, finishing his round with a pocketful of fresh, velvety pelts worth twopence each.

As the marchers climbed, skirting the 2,000-foot High Pike, the clouds lifted to give glorious views over the Solway Firth to the north, and sweeping green slopes to the south. 'God's own country,' said a deep Cumbrian voice at one brief halt. 'But if hunting's stopped, He'll be the only one up here.' Another farmer remarked that hunting is the least, not most, cruel means of pest-control: 'Fox is either dead, or clean away. He can't be wounded.' Someone else spoke of the tension between hunting and shooting fraternities, and how the fell packs regard anyone who shoots foxes with positive disfavour. Barry Todhunter agreed that if hunting were banned, the fox would be far worse off: 'There'd be an absolute free-for-all. Every man jack who could carry a gun or set a snare would be out here after him, and the fox would be pretty well exterminated. The natural harmony and balance in this part of the world would be overthrown.'

Still moving fast, the column went over a pass, dropped through heather to a stream, climbed again on to an old miners' track which followed the contour across a steep face – an outlying slope of Skiddaw. Presently Derwentwater came into sight, lying like a sheet of pewter in one of the valleys ahead, and although the peaks were still in cloud, some of the marchers were remembering how, in Macaulay's ringing line, 'the red glow on Skiddaw roused the burghers of Carlisle,' when the Spanish Armada threatened England. In the summer of 1588 a chain of beacons had sent news of the attempted invasion flaring northwards; now, four centuries later, news of a different kind was travelling south.

The lunch-stop, that first day, was typical of many that followed. With boundless generosity, local volunteers had loaded their cars with drinks, sandwiches, pies, sausage rolls, slices of quiche and other sustaining delights, and driven up to the spot where a lane ends on a shoulder above Keswick. Having covered fourteen miles in good time, the walkers were glad to sink down on the grass with food and drink to hand. Several were already in trouble with blisters, not least Gary Bell, the only man to come over from Northern Ireland, whose trainers had rubbed his feet raw in a single morning.

Setting off again refreshed, the core walkers plunged down the steep hill into Keswick, where they wheeled left into the grounds of the hospital to pay their respects to George Bell, who hunted the Blencathra hounds from 1931 to 1949. Now a spry and smartly-turned-out ninety-five, George was waiting for them in the car-park: he clearly enjoyed the sudden arrival of a mass of yellow shirts, and when someone asked for the secret of his longevity, he answered, with brilliant simplicity, 'Go oop fell.'

That evening brought another long climb, over Newlands Hause, the border between Blencathra country and its neighbour, the

Melbreak. By the time the walkers came wearily down into Buttermere, at 5.30pm, they had more than twenty miles of steep country behind them. Everyone agreed they had gone too fast, but everyone was thrilled to hear that Barry Todhunter – who walked for his living, and spent every winter scurrying about those fells – had developed a blister.

The second day's leg, from Buttermere to Ambleside, struck through the highest, roughest fell country: climb out through Scarth Gap pass, pass Haystacks, drop into Ennerdale, climb again over Black Sail pass, then over Kirk Fell and down to Wasdale Head. After a late lunch the walkers faced another long ascent to Sty Head tarn and on to Esk Hause, 2,490 feet high, before dropping past Rossett Pike and down Mickleden into Langdale. By the end of that punishing day blisters had became one of the main topics of conversation. Almost everybody suffered from them sooner or later, and protracted discussions smouldered on about the relative merits of boots and trainers. John Harrison set off in his normal hunting gear – heavy, leather boots, with soles turned up at the front to lift the wearer up steep slopes. These were fine on the fells, but on roads they proved so uncomfortable that when he reached Penrith he bought a pair of lighter walking boots.

On tarmac most people found training shoes the better bet: boots transmitted too much shock, and trainers, with softer soles and more insulation, jarred the wearer less. Many marchers found that their best policy was to switch from one to the other at the midday halt, so as to change, however slightly, the points at which their feet came under maximum pressure. On dull days or in the rain, walking on roads was quite comfortable, but when the sun beat down and heated up the tarmac, it felt (as one man put it) 'as though your soles were on fire.'

If no single character emerged clearly on the first couple of days, there was one man who stood out purely by virtue of his appearance. Nobody could have looked less like the popular image of a fox-hunter than Dave Brearley, a thirty-one-year old, self-employed pest-control operator from North Yorkshire. Painfully thin, with a shaven head (but sporting a wavy moustache), he was immediately noticeable because his neck and the sides of his head were covered in tattoos. The words DRUNK PUNK ran round one side of his neck, and all over his throat stretched a spider's web – something which, in due course, inevitably led to him becoming known as Spiderman, or Spiderman Dave.

Because he was rather shy, and had little self-confidence, it took fellow walkers some time to discover his curious history. Together with three younger brothers, he was brought up on a small holding, from which his father ran a one-man pest-control service. From the age of five he was keen on ferreting rabbits, shooting rats with a .22 and so on; but at eleven he began going to parties and drinking alcohol, and he had no interest in any more education, or in the gamekeepers' course which his father planned he should take.

All he wanted was to escape into the big city – Leeds – and this he did at sixteen. By then it was 1981, the height of the punk rock movement, so he got himself a Mohican hair-cut, had his nose and one ear pierced, and went seriously on the booze, drinking himself insensible every day. (It was while unconscious that he got his tattoos, from an artist practising on his inert body.) More and more often he found himself in hospital or in court, and he started going to prison for alcohol-induced offences: shoplifting, theft, fighting.

When he tired of the city, he pitched up on travellers' communal sites all over the country, living in tents, vans and buses. One reason he sought out such places was that many of the 'lost and lonely people' on those sites also had drink or drug problems; but the main attraction was that he felt more comfortable back in his native element, the countryside.

It was during that period that he had his first contact with the antis – the Animal Liberation Front, the League Against Cruel Sports and the Hunt Saboteurs' Association. Representatives often came round the travellers' sites offering £20 for a day's sabbing or protesting outside laboratories, and among the young down-and-outs, who had no direction in their lives, it was easy for them to pick up recruits. As Dave recalls, 'they had no problem filling their Transit vans, because £20 meant you could feed your addiction for a day.'

He himself never succumbed to the antis' blandishments – and indeed he always stuck out as someone slightly strange, because he kept a terrier and a lurcher, and usually some ferrets, and while his companions ate their lentils and veggie-burgers, he would be working his way through rabbit stew.

He eventually laid off alcohol in May 1992 after he had nearly killed himself by crashing a van while drunk: as it was, he smashed his left leg so badly that surgeons proposed to amputate the limb, until he was saved by a specialist who rebuilt it with plates, rods and bolts. After six months in hospital, he took himself to Warwick University, got a diploma in pest control, and set up his own small business. He also started to work with suffering or reformed alcoholics, through visits to probation courts and prisons, public lectures and radio talks.

An unusual customer, then, but a man of high value to the marches, for he had seen both sides of the field-sports argument and come out emphatically in favour. Moreover, his appearance was a godsend. Already it had caused delight at Caldbeck – when he appeared in the Oddfellows Arms on the first evening, someone shouted, 'Ey-oop! Here comes bloody Swampy!' – and he was the butt of frequent cracks about people tunnelling under airport runways and building huts in trees. More seriously, on the march, if trouble from antis ever loomed or materialised, he could be sent forward to disarm it, and in places where there seemed to be a particular threat, he led the column.

It took some time for his colleagues to appreciate that this rather withdrawn man hated his tattoos – the spider's web above all – and that he was in constant pain from the metal in his shattered leg. When they saw him labouring, they might offer him a squirt of WD 40 to ease his joints, but after a while they realised that he had been through hell and come out with exceptional inner strength.

It had cost him dear to join the march at all. Living from week to week, 'sometimes from job to job,' he had had to withdraw his entire savings – about £400 – to buy two new pairs of Berghaus Goretex walking boots and other necessities, leaving his wife Kate short of funds to run the house and look after their two baby daughters. Yet he felt he had no option but to go, for he 'could not stand even to think about my children or grandchildren looking through history and nature books and asking, "Daddy – what was a foxhound? What was a working terrier? What was a grouse? What was ferreting? What was a gamekeeper?"' The idea moved him so strongly that his eyes would fill just thinking about it.

Many of the core walkers were making similar or greater financial sacrifices. John Harrison could have been earning £300 a week at his summer work of fencing or building dry-stone walls – and it was galling for him to miss it, because, with European Community grants on offer, his friends were building walls everywhere. 'Nineteen pounds per square metre!' he exclaimed. 'It's money for jam.'

Gary Bell had forgone the chance of driving a catering firm's van round race-tracks in the south of England: that, together with his air fare from Belfast, had cost him at least £1,000. Some people were marching to protect their jobs, others (like Spiderman Dave) so that their children would not inherit an impoverished, emasculated countryside more like a theme-park than a natural environment; but all were marching for freedom of choice and the right to determine their own future.

The second half of the northern contingent left Coldstream on 15 June, one day after the start at Caldbeck. The night before, there had been a brief panic, when Sam Butler received a telephone call in the Marches Office from Sergeant Sandy Walker of the North Yorkshire police. He had heard that some event was due to take place at Coldstream in the morning, but he had no details. Somehow the information sent out by Butler had failed to percolate downwards; but when he put through a call at 10.35 that night, the sergeant took the news with admirable equanimity. 'Oh,' he said, 'don't worry. I expect details will reach us with the stage coach comes in tomorrow morning.'

Again it was dull and grey, but at least no rain was falling as the core walkers and hangers-on assembled at the entrance to the Hirsel, ancestral home of the Douglas-Home family. Some people were slightly disappointed by the turn-out of supporters – only about 250 – but all worries fell away as two pipers led the column along the main street, skirling out 'Scotland the Brave', and when they headed south over the bridge into England, the powerful associations of the setting combined with excitement and nervousness to set tears rolling down many cheeks, male as well as female. Just ahead of the column, across its bows, a single swan flew down the Tweed from right to left, heading like a white arrow for the sea: to many, a sign of freedom.

One party of day-walkers had made an extraordinary effort to take part. A posse of deer-stalkers and ghillies had left Kinbrace, in

Sutherland, at 1 am and driven through the night to reach Coldstream in time for the start. But because their transport was the school bus, which would be needed for the run on Monday morning, they were able to walk for only a couple of hours, to the mid-morning break, before piling back into the vehicle and heading north again.

Those who had done military service inevitably found themselves thinking of General George Monck, who in January 1660 marched his own regiment from Coldstream to London down this very road. He too had come over that bridge, probably to the sound of fife and drum. Monck had been a supporter of Oliver Cromwell during the Civil War, and prominent in the Protector's Irish campaigns; but since Cromwell's death in 1658 he had swung round to support the restoration of the monarch, King Charles II. After the failure of Cromwell's successor, his ineffective son Richard ('Tumbledown Dick'), Monck became determined that the army, which had effectively been in control of the country, should be reconciled with Parliament, and that free parliamentary elections should be held. The King was still in exile, in Holland, but in December 1659 Monck was appointed Commander-in-Chief of the army, and 1 January 1660 he set off for London to provide a bodyguard for the monarch, when he returned.

Considering what one contemporary called 'the foulness of the ways,' and the fact that the ground was covered with snow for the whole distance, so that when the men reached the south they 'had scarce yet seen the plain earth of their native country', they made remarkably good time, marching into the City of London on 3 February – a transit of thirty-four days. After the restoration, in May 1660, the King rewarded Monck by creating his regiment the Coldstream Guards.

Leading the latter-day march was a man of distinct military bearing: thirty-year-old Edward Tate, who had served ten years in the Welsh Guards, finishing as a captain. Tall, slim, straightforward in looks and manner, with a precise, rather buttoned-up way of talking, he had become a self-employed builder, working from his home in Wiltshire and hunting keenly with the VWH. Like many fellow-walkers, he had been feeling for at least two years that countrymen needed to stage some major protest, and that if they

40

did, it should embrace issues far wider than merely hunting; but it was a chance meeting with Charles Mann, at a cocktail party near home, that had given him his opening. Mann quickly sensed that here was a man who would not only walk all the way from Scotland to London, but would also make a first-class leader; so he sounded him out, and within a couple of days Tate had signed on.

The prospect of walking twenty miles a day for twenty days, and of leading a small army down the road to Hyde Park, did not daunt him. For one thing, he himself was fit from constantly scrambling around building sites, up and down scaffolding, day-in, day-out. For another, some years earlier he had walked from Liverpool to Cardiff with a party of schoolchildren, soldiers and wheelchair-bound tetraplegics, to raise money for an orthopaedic hospital and a charity called The Western Spirit which runs youth hostels in Cardiff, Liverpool and Newcastle-upon-Tyne. On that occasion he had been on the road for a week, covering nearly thirty miles a day, and he had been amazed by the resilience and determination of the young people.

Now, in 1997, he soon established a routine: press, radio and television interviews from 8.30 am, a nine-o'clock start, a drinks break around 11 am, a buffet lunch for the 20-odd core walkers, laid on by well-wishers, at 1pm, a tea-break about 3.30 pm, and the finish some time after 5pm. At the end of each march local people offering accommodation would meet the marchers, and Tate would allocate his people to the various houses or other shelters on offer. At first, when he scarcely knew anybody, his distribution was random; but as the walkers began to fall into groups, and he read their characters and backgrounds more clearly, he split them up as he felt most appropriate. Each batch would then go off with their hosts for the evening, to have a bath or shower and change their clothes. In the course of the march he himself slept in many fine houses, but also in a Wendy house, a barn, a conservatory, and once, when there was nowhere else, under the stars.

Supper would sometimes be at individual houses, sometimes at central barbecues. Hospitality ran at such a level that it soon became a problem: ravenous though they were, the walkers could not do justice to the mountains of food set before them. The Highland contingent soon had a joke about whisky up and

41

running. One evening Mark Naisby, from Inveraray, asked his host if he had 'any old whisky that needed drinking up,' and thereafter the hunt was on for old whisky that ought to be drunk for fear that it might go off. Whereever they landed, the marchers always found they had much in common with their hosts, who, like them, were engaged in every kind of country pursuit – farming, growing trees, producing rare breeds, gardening, breeding terriers, walking foxhounds.

The start of the third leg, at Weldon, was disrupted by a sudden furore of press interest. The afternoon before, Michael Foster had announced in London that he would bring in his bill to ban hunting that day – 17 June. The news certainly lent the crusade fresh urgency, but it seemed that every newspaper and television station in the country wanted interviews with the marchers. GMTV asked for a spokesman to talk about hunting, and after some discussion, Tate put forward George Bowyer, sometime estate agent, MFH, computer expert and insurance broker, to talk not only about hunting, but about the countryside as a whole. Then, late in the morning as the column approached Morpeth, it was hit by a ferocious storm: stair-rods of rain interspersed with hailstones. Depressing though this was, many walkers preferred it to blazing sunshine, for the worst enemy was heat, and provided people could keep moving, they did not much mind being wet. Yet for the farmers in the column it was depressing to see wheat beaten flat by the storm, and strawberries sodden with rain.

Before long Tate – who reminded one colleague of 'an overgrown schoolboy' – became the object of gentle mockery. Most mornings, before departure, he would climb on to the bonnet of a Land Rover to address the day-walkers and give them a briefing on safety: walk not more than three-abreast, watch out for themselves and those around them, pay attention to the stewards' instructions, and so on. He also reminded them that the media would be about, and said that if any press, radio or television people appeared, the walkers should 'ask them to pop up the column and see me, Ed Tate – that's myself, Edward Tate.' These words became the march's slogan: the moment Tate stepped up to give his morning brief, or when he had just finished, there would be a derisive roar of 'ED TATE. THAT'S MYSELF, EDWARD TATE!'

To some of the marchers he became known as 'Myself' – but the teasing was essentially good-natured, and soon everyone recognised him as an outstanding leader, selfless, thoughtful, calm, and a first-rate organiser.

His column contained many men and women with exceptional qualities, but nobody showed greater courage than Derek Cross, a gardener and sheep-farmer from Gloucestershire. Heavily built, and in his late forties, Cross was severely impeded by osteo-arthritis, and waiting for operations to replace both hips: he moved awkwardly, with knees and toes turned in, and when other marchers first saw him, they could not believe that it was physically possible for him to survive one whole day, let alone 400 miles.

By sheer guts, he did – even though he had to walk with his eyes fixed on the road a few yards ahead, concentrating intently. Within a few minutes of each day's start he would have beads of sweat standing out on his forehead, from the sheer effort he was having to make, and some of his colleagues found it too painful even to watch him struggling. As one of them put it, 'He was dead on his feet before Morpeth.' To Ed Tate he was 'a remarkable man. If any of us thought we were sore or in pain, we only had to look at Derek and imagine what he was going through. Then we'd realise that our own problems were pretty insignificant.' As they went further south, Tate would use a joke about Derek's extraordinary fortitude to wake up day-walkers who had just joined. 'He's waiting for an operation,' he would tell them, 'and his doctor asked him to go on a short constitutional walk. He started it ten days ago in Coldstream, and he's still going.'

One factor which helped Derek along was the close companionship which developed between him and three other marchers, Dave Clement, Paul Crofts and Nathan Oldham. The first to befriend him was Clement, a big, well-built deer-stalker with close-cropped hair and a moustache. A native of the Lake District, but now working at Forsinard, far in the northern wilds of Sutherland, Clement quickly became famous from the fact that he walked in green Wellington boots. Admittedly they were of high quality – Le Chameau, lined with leather and costing nearly £200 – but nobody understood how he could tolerate anything so hot and uncomfortable on his feet. When challenged, he retorted that at home he covered fifteen miles a day in wellies, and couldn't see that this walk was going to be any different. On the first day, when he did try trainers, they promptly gave him blisters, and he reverted to the boots for the rest of the 400 miles to London.

At thirty-four, Wellies Dave was a dozen years younger than Derek, but he took the older man under his wing and gave him endless friendly encouragement, staying with him when he fell back, nursing him along with psychological support. Another who did the same was Nathan Oldham, a bearded ghillie from Borrobol, also in Sutherland: he too formed a close bond with the sufferer. The third man who helped was Paul Crofts, a hill fox-hunter from Inverness-shire who rarely spoke but showed a such a sure propensity for setting a good pace that, from Day One, he became the march's front man: having volunteered for the job, he did it perfectly.

The experience of walking through Wales had shown Ed Tate how vital it was that the pace should be right. From the start at Coldstream the column went off rather too fast, but after lunch, with Paul in the lead, it settled to an easy speed of not much over three miles per hour. The next day, Tate had the idea of putting Paul, Derek and Dave together at the head of the column, and this had the excellent effect of slowing everyone down: on some days brakes were needed particularly for the marchers' hosts, who joined the core walkers and liked to set off at a brisk canter.

At the start of the walk fitness levels varied greatly. The Highlanders were in good shape anyway, from the amount of exercise they took at their work, and they had done no special training (Dave Clement described his period of preparation as 'seventeen years' – his working life). Others walked furiously to get fit – and none harder than John Morris, a schoolmaster and former Royal Naval officer living in Kent. At fifty-eight, he was the oldest man on the Scottish march, and received details of the enterprise only ten days before the start:

> Finishing breakfast, I immediately set off to walk ten miles in my sturdy, everyday working shoes. Returning with mildly aching feet, but no blisters or other physical damage, I felt I just about had the time to work up to twenty miles per day by the starting

date, and phoned the Marches' Office to offer my services as a core walker.

The next day, having bathed my feet in surgical spirit, I covered a further twelve miles, to return with a blister on the ball of my left foot which, after treatment with that ever-faithful medicament, caused me some discomfort but no significant pain. However, fourteen miles the following day produced a further blister on the raw flesh of the existing one, which rendered me almost incapable of putting my foot to the ground. Thankfully, I had a previous commitment to three days' sailing in the Channel . . .

On my return my elder son, a veteran of the French Foreign Legion and an intrepid mountaineer, introduced me to Compeed blister plasters, which cover the blister with a layer of simulated skin. Thus treated, and wearing my hiking boots, I embarked on a tentative six miles, which I completed without a problem, followed, a day later, by a further uninjurious twelve miles. I had promised my son, who had broken his leg after leaving a perfectly serviceable aeroplane at 2,000 feet, that I would mow his lawns; and so the day before leaving for Scotland saw me walking the nineteen miles from my home to fulfil this commitment.

This rigorous preparation, which Morris considered 'the bare minimum,' in the end did him proud, and he had no serious foot trouble the whole way to London. (It was left to others, who shared rooms with him, to record that he was a 'world-class snorer.') Sarah Morley, a Yorkshire farmer's wife, also took her training seriously, and covered between four and ten miles a day for six weeks. Richard Markham, a hunt servant from the Belvoir kennels in Lincolnshire, put in one training walk of eighteen miles and three of ten.

Less provident starters were soon suffering from blisters, and the ebullient Colonel Reggie Purbrick, a former Lancer, now farming near Oakham, was elected what he called 'the team vet,' being called upon to treat 'blisters of varying horror', as well as sore shins and aching knees. Purbrick quickly became one of the column's stars, frequently making idiotic remarks to cheer people up.

'Everyone started taking the piss out of him,' John Harrison recorded, 'and good on him, he stood every inch of it.' On the third evening out from Coldstream he composed a brief memorandum – 'HELPFUL TIPS FROM REGGIE' – for despatch to the marches office and onward transmission to coördinators farther south. This included the following advice:

FEEDING
These core walkers need meat and two veg. If a barbecue is on offer, perhaps the core walkers ought to have a plate of stew first? They are expending a huge amount of energy every day, and only have a snack lunch. Good breakfast essential. Much as we would like to, we can't handle a party *every* night!

ACCOMMODATION
I am seriously concerned that thirty-four people is a lot to put up.* But I have to say, these people really seem to need a bath fast on completion of the day's march. No panic for those who are putting people up in village halls etc., but let them be aware. At the moment the weather is so vile (good for walking but very cold if you stand around for more than a minute) that I have deemed (as Flo Nightingale) all to be casualties at the end of the day, and therefore to be removed to hosts forthwith-ish!

Well-meant as it was, Reggie's advice did not find favour everywhere down the line: hosts had already made arrangements, and were loath to change them. Nevertheless, vast amounts of meat did begin to appear at evening meals, and some marchers got the impression that their entertainment had been needlessly curtailed. In George Bowyer's view, 'Sometimes the policy seemed to be: a bowl of stew and dumplings, and straight to bed.'

On the stage from south of Weldon to Belsay, in Northumberland, the self-appointed guide for the day was the marchers' host, Major Roddy 'Bang-On' Bailey, Master of the Percy, who set such a cracking pace that other walkers were relieved when, in mid-afternoon, he announced that there were only two more miles to

*He was looking ahead to the time when the Lakeland and Coldstream columns joined, raising the combined total of core walkers to thirty-four.

the kennels and the end of the leg. An hour later, having breezed along at a good four miles per hour, he cheerfully declared that there was only a mile and a half to go. A further hour later, the column eventually staggered to its destination – and as one marcher remarked, 'It wasn't clear whether the epithet "Bang-On" reflected Roddy's judgement of distance or his prowess as a raconteur. However, thereafter any mention of distance-to-go elicited a chorus of "Is that imperial miles or Bailey miles?" '

Banter bounced up and down the column, a good deal of it generated by or about the irrepressible Reggie, and occasional cheerful remarks from people they passed helped the marchers on their way. On 19 June, as they crossed the Tyne at Stocksfield, with 300 miles ahead of them, an old boy stood at the end of the bridge and shouted, 'Well done, lads! You'll not have far to go now. You're south!' That day brought them level with the town of Jarrow, a few miles down-river to the east, and Ed Tate's thoughts turned again to the march of 1936. Comparisons with that famous event were by no means far-fetched, he decided: 'Jarrow was about jobs – and nearly half the people walking with us would be out of a job if country sports were banned. Their families would be thrown out of their houses. Their lives would change for ever, as would their environment, the countryside.'

Next day in the former mining areas of Durham – the land of the pigeon fanciers – a man told of a friend who had had his racing birds liberated by animal-rights fanatics, because they believed that racing was stressful. 'They took birds to what they reckoned was a place of safety and let them off,' the man recounted happily. 'You can guess what happened. Booggers came straight back, didn't they?'

Unknown to most of his fellows, Dave Clement was keeping up his habitual diary, and this reflected the occasional social stress that he was feeling. At a briefing the night before the march started, he had been disconcerted to find that he and Paul Crofts were expected to act as marshals on the road, and to help deal with the press. He was not happy when the organisers cautioned core walkers to be careful about how they talked to the press, because it seemed to him that the bosses were trying to run the march in their own interests 'or at least in the upper classes' interests for their sport.' Further south, he was disgusted by an MFH who 'didn't ever talk properly to any of us' and then pronounced that 'hunt servants are not capable of judging hounds.'

More often, though, his journal recorded the physical struggle on the road: 'Derek battling on admirably! TC, total commitment . . . Long, slow, painful afternoon dragging Derek on. Even had to sing Lakeland hunting songs to him down the mile straight before finishing . . . Core walkers not keen to break the rhythm for drink stops. Just wanting to march on.'

Food and drink were also much on his mind: 'Lasagne and spuds. Pudding available, but I couldn't face any . . . [At dinner] full leg of the finest fat lamb, mountain of pavlova . . . Unbelievable support from hunt wives: strawberries, bananas, drinks etc.' A particularly memorable lunch-stop was the one laid on by the Braes of Derwent hunt at the Queen's Head in Lanchester, during the twenty-four mile stretch from Whittonstall to Durham: 'Coffee at the Chinese restaurant, then the biggest piece of steak-and-kidney pie, Yorkshire pudding, chips and veg. Only Nathan and Mark ate it all, and even they had some leftovers.'

After five or six days, people had got to know each other, and the column settled down into groups of kindred souls. Yet even if particular friendships developed, a formidable sense of common purpose united the whole party. Dick Tonks, a forty-year-old terrier man from Selby in North Yorkshire, had spent twenty years in the mining industry, and thought he would never find such comradeship again – but here it was, stronger than anything he had known. He was thrilled by the sense 'of belonging to a real force. Whether it was a lord or a sir or a coursing lad we met, we all had one thing in common – our love of the countryside.'

Most of the walkers, when asked why they signed on, gave answers like 'To do something for our sport . . . To secure my job . . . A desire to make some practical contribution to the cause.' Peter Jones-Davies, a retired army officer, had risen to 'the challenge of walking 400 miles at the age of fifty-three.' Archie Clapton and his sister Joanna, students from Ayrshire, both saw 'a good chance to put something back into field-sports, having got so much pleasure from them as children.'

But Henry Hudson, a tall, cheerful, long-striding young sales-man from Lincolnshire, was refreshingly honest about his non-conservationist motives: 'I spotted the potential for a good time, lots of new faces, good booze and food, all the pretty young girls . . . Need I say more?' An older marcher recorded that Henry wore shorts throughout, 'and completed the march with mahogany-coloured legs, which lit up the eyes of even the not-so-young females.' Sarah Morley, the farmer's wife who trained so rigor-ously, claimed that she had 'volunteered while under the influence, and had to go through with it.' Nevertheless, she was also driven by the firm conviction that 'country people know what is best for the countryside.' As the march progressed, she grew increasingly articulate about the ideas it was expressing: she became one of the column's most effective spokesmen, and at the end was rewarded by being chosen as one of the delegation to go by bus from the Hyde Park rally to Downing Street.

Naturally there were setbacks. Shaun Vickers, a factory worker and coursing enthusiast from Co. Durham, had given up the chance of a £250-a-week job in order to walk, but on the first day he received a telephone call from his girl-friend, saying that her horse had died. He therefore had to travel home that night and rejoin the march later. (He was only moderately amused by the way his friend Dick Tonks insisted on introducing him to strangers: 'This is Shaun Vickers, the poacher'). A larger-scale problem occurred at Durham on 20 June, when the day's walk was scheduled to end at Houghhall, the agricultural college – an ideal rendezvous, as it was off the road and had plenty of parking space. At the last moment the principal of the college announced that he did not want to play host to the marchers, as he considered them 'too political.' This did not go down at all well with local farmers, who regularly took students from the college for work experience on their land; but the obstruction caused little trouble, because the column merely carried on 300 yards down the road to a pub, where the people made them warmly welcome.

Such rebuffs were rare. Expecting 'perhaps two V-signs a day from passing motorists,' Ed Tate found that many days passed without a single gesture of disapproval. On the contrary, antis were conspicuous by their absence, and all down the road the marchers were encouraged by the friendly reactions of the natives. A basic tenet of the walkers' code was that they should show courtesy to everyone they met or passed, and almost always their overtures were reciprocated with a smile, a wave, a few words of encouragement or a merry toot on the horn. As Tate remarked, 'The only chance we had of making a personal impression on people was when we were on the road. Our banners and T-shirts helped, but our big weapon was to behave in a dignified and orderly manner, and to give everyone a smile.'

Once they were into the swing of it, many people simply enjoyed the walking, and the beauty of the landscape through which they were slowly passing. Peter Jones-Davies felt 'the joy of being a private soldier, not an officer, and thus having no responsibilities, duties or worries.' The further he went, the more clearly he saw that the abolition of hunting would be a 'waste of history, tradition and centuries of hard work and effort.' Tradition was celebrated most evenings in the form of hunting songs and dancing, in pubs, halls, tents or on farm trailers. Familiar Lakeland ditties were augmented by 'The Countryside Song', composed and sung by George Bowyer, which admirably expressed what the marches were all about – 'Oh, what a pity! Oh, what a shame! Someone is trying to ban country sports again'. (The full text is given in Appendix A. Bowyer had written half the song some time before the marches began, and he composed the rest of it in his head as he drove the Coldstream column's support van up the A1 towards the start – a task not rendered any easier by the fact that he had two loquacious core marchers on board.)

On Monday, 23 June, the Caldbeck and Coldstream columns united at Northallerton – and a great moment it was. For Wils Boow, a civil servant who had walked all the way from Carlisle, 'it was really something, quite spectacular, to see the two marches coming in from opposite ends of the street and meeting in the middle.' His partner Sue Elms thought it 'a brilliant and very emotional moment,' and Sarah Morley found it equally moving: 'As we came down from the north, and the Lakes boys from the south, the town was full of people, and the main street echoed to the sound of holloa-ing and hunting horns.'

Among the crowd gathered to greet them was Kate Brearley, Dave's wife, who had brought along their daughters Leveret (two)

and Lakota (eleven months). The company quickly repaired to the
Golden Lion – and it was then that there occurred one of the
march's few untoward incidents. Someone came into the pub, told
Brearley that a couple of antis were causing trouble outside, and
asked him to remonstrate. 'They'd just kicked one of the vans
carrying our gear, and they were getting a bit abusive,' he recalls:

> I went out and found a young lass with her boyfriend, shouting
> and bawling about how hunting was an upper-class pursuit for
> toffs and stuck-up people. I went across and said, 'Eh – how can
> you call ME stuck-up and upper-class? Am I a f – g toff?' The lass
> kept chuntering on about this, that and other, but eventually I
> started getting sense through to her. It turned out she was a
> farmer's daughter, and she was all right, smiling-ish. You could
> talk sense to her. But the lad just didn't want to listen. He was
> going ballistic, off his head, really stoned. You could have put an
> artic. in front of him, and he wouldn't have noticed.

With the trouble defused, the combined column headed south, now
thirty-four core marchers strong. Still Paul Crofts led, nursing
Derek Cross along, and John Harrison, freed from any need to
regulate the pace, ranged up and down talking to one person after
another. Paul Steel, one of the most formidable of the Lakeland
team, burnt off his inexhaustible energy by acting as a high-velocity
steward.

For many, the high spot of the journey was their stay at
Ravenswick, home of Mary Holt and her husband James near
Kirkbymoorside, north of York. The hospitality offered by the
Holts in their rambling farmhouse extended over two nights, either
side of a rest-day, and was by any standards prodigious. The
marchers ate colossal amounts of food, much of it provided by hunt
supporters and friends – Mary had never seen people eat like it. But
what made it unforgettable was the walkers' initiation into that
desperate game (or form of warfare), fireball hockey.

Mary, a middle-aged woman who described herself as a 'lapsed
housewife and portrait painter,' was about to join the march
herself, and for the past month had been walking five fast miles
every day to get fit. As a final warm-up, after a lavish dinner, she

produced several bottles of port and advised her guests to tank up well before the start of the midnight contest. Her husband confirmed that the game, which had originated on the West Coast of Scotland, was too alarming to be played by anyone sober.

Until then the Holt family had played with garden forks; but the men from the north had pronounced this intolerably dangerous, so that morning Mary had been into town and bought sixteen new hockey sticks. Now teams were selected. Mary thought she had done well by bagging several of the macho Lakesmen, but the opposing skipper, Rowena Hudson from Durham University, had craftily signed up real hockey players, past or present, from the ranks of the Coldstreamers. The new sticks were handed out, and on the lower lawn, in pitch darkness, the game began. John Morris gave a vivid description of the scene:

The ball was a toilet roll wrapped in chicken wire and soaked in petrol. It flew back and forth like a demented meteorite, but the more adroit Coldstreamers quickly assumed control and were soon in a commanding lead. Each chukka lasted about five minutes, ending when the ball burnt out and another was lit.

By half-time it was clear that the rules of hockey had been superseded by jungle law, and a surreptitious blow in the face reduced my spectacles to two pieces. During the interval Dave Brearley saturated a tea-towel in water and wrapped it round one hand. At the re-start the ball flew towards the Lakes' goal, as usual, but Dave snatched it up and ran towards the Coldstreamers' end. Unfortunately he had reckoned without our goalie, Anthony (the Eating Machine) Warmington, who not only filled the space between the posts, but overflowed it.

The sad outcome was that the ball burned through the tea-towel before Dave could score – and he still bears the scars. Even the introduction of a shovel could not reverse the Lakesmen's slide, and the final score was 5 – 2, a pair of broken glasses, two burned hands and miscellaneous scorched shoes, trousers and shirts.

At his alfresco surgery next morning, Reggie Purbrick for once dealt with more burns than blisters. Heading south, Mary joined the column, and at first John Harrison thought she would last a couple of days at the most, as she was finding it difficult to keep up. 'You'll get the swing of it,' he told her – and sure enough, next day she came waltzing by him, never to look back. Alone of the core marchers she brought her car with her, leaving it at the start-point each day and getting a lift back with one of the day-walkers to collect it in the evening. On board, apart from her personal belongings, were the sixteen new sticks, in case the chance should arise for another game of fireball hockey.

As the column approached York, it was swollen by day-walkers to nearly 100 people, and on the northern fringes of the city there occurred one of the few major changes of plan. The original aim had been to slip through York along the cycle path which follows the river: Bob Hyde, the local co-ordinator, had done a tremendous amount of work devising a route which would cause minimal disruption of traffic. But in the suburbs a call came up to the front of the column, asking Ed Tate if he would reconsider and go through the city-centre instead. He and Bob immediately thought, 'Why not?' and after a brief Chinese parliament saw that everyone was in favour of changing course. The point, after all, was that as many citizens as possible should see the marchers and get their message, and already some people felt that they had been excessively cautious about avoiding centres of population. They had by-passed several large towns, because the organisers had thought it wise to avoid any risk of creating traffic jams.

In the view of Sam Butler, 'this was one of those inspirational decisions.' The marchers formed into a column only two abreast, and walked quietly through the centre, past the Minster and other historic buildings. For many, the experience proved one of the trip's highlights. Earlier that day the gloomy weather had depressed morale, and John Harrison found that the passage through York 'brightened the day no end.' It also made the organisers in the south realise that passage through towns was perfectly feasible.

Morale was hardly ever low – and if one or two people sometimes felt down, there were others on a high to lift them up. The odds were that anyone prepared to walk 400 miles was fairly strong-minded – not to say bloody-minded – and unlikely to give in to the pain of blisters or sore shins. On rest days, some swam and lazed about, others went fishing; but the great delight of the hunting folk was to visit the kennels of whatever pack they were passing through, and for William Wakeham, thirty-year-old Master of the Eglinton, the highlight of the whole journey was 'finding an Eglinton line in the Grove & Rufford kennels.'

Dave Brearley had been telephoning home every morning and evening, but one night, when he came through, his wife Kate burst into tears. Bills were pouring in – final demands, court threats about missed payments. With Dave away, everything had piled on top of her. Dave felt bad that he was not at home to tackle the problems, but when he offered to return there and then, she said fiercely, 'NO! Carry on walking.' All he could do was tell her not to worry about the demands. 'Look, love,' he said. 'They might cut off the electric and the phone. I can sort that out when I get back. But if Michael Foster's bill goes through, we won't have a chance, because I won't have a job any more.' When he called again in the morning, Kate had cheered up, and told him he'd taken the right decision.

On the march went, through Yorkshire, Nottinghamshire and Leicestershire, from Scrooby to Laxton, from Laxton to Staunton-in-the-Vale, from Staunton-in-the-Vale to Wymondham, from Wymondham to Caldecott, through or past the countries of celebrated hunts – the Belvoir, the Quorn, the Cottesmore, the Fernie, the Pytchley, the Grafton, the Bicester. Agreeable twinges of nostalgia assailed Ed Tate as he passed through the Cottesmore country, for his grandfather had been master of the hunt, and in Oakham he was delighted to meet Fred Mills, his grandfather's old stud groom.

All the way new jokes sprang into being, old-established characters consolidated their reputations, and new ones emerged. The genial Gary Bell from Ulster was well established as the man who never passed a pub without going in, and also as a demon after old whisky that needed finishing. When he spotted a bottle on the back seat of a car, out in the country miles from anywhere, he became known as the Man Who Found Whisky from Nowhere.

On 1 June the lunch-stop in Newark market was greatly enhanced by the arrival of Nell Stroud, ring-mistress of the Santus

Fell men. Back row from left: Paul Steel, John Harrison, Mike Nicholson, Richard Akrigg, Dave Brearley. Front: Gary Bell, Wilson Boow.

Mark Selway leads off Dartmoor.

Top: Cornish marchers Amie Pascoe (left) Neil Mathieson (centre) Peter Webb (right). Below: outside the Golden Lion, Northallerton. Ed Tate (left), Gary Bell (right) and Dave Brearley with daughter Leveret.

The Highland Gang. Back row: Dave Clement, Mark Naisby, Piper, Derek Cross. Front: Carl Naisby, Paul Croft, Nathan Oldham.

Cornish marchers. Jackie and Michael Allway, and June Moon

Peter Richards from the Tregurtha stud, Penzance, presents a Cornish pasty to walkers June Moon, Brian Webber, Sam Taylor (rear) and Alethea Bick at the start of the walk, Madron, Cornwall.

David and Jo Latham.

Crowds greet the Welsh marchers at Stow-on-the-Wold.

David Jones at Stow (Sam Butler, right).   *Simon Clarke, New Forest.*

Jeremy Irons addresses the rally in Hyde Park.

A Cornish demonstration of feet en route.

Sue Morgan and Richard Jones.

Circus, who appeared in tiara, red tail coat, fishnet tights and full circus make-up, riding a coloured stallion. One or two purists were none too pleased, considering her dress a caricature of hunting costume; but Nell herself was so taken with enthusiasm for the walkers' cause that she promised all possible support, even to the extent of mobilising elephants for another march – should there be one – and in due course she appeared on the stand at the Hyde Park rally. The entries in Dave Clement's diary make it clear that many of the march's rigours were self-induced:

Thursday, 3 July. I got lost going to bed, ended up in the sherriff's room. Time for a sharp exit. Woke Nathan 7 am to go for a swim. Told not to take no for an answer, so dragged him out. Cool job until we got in, cold job getting out. Full breakfast, more sausages available, only three dished out each. Managed to eat and enjoy it all.

Set off from the pub near Wymondham at the usual time, bound for the Cottesmore kennels at coffee time. Ed's brief there got a laugh . . . Walked past Rutland Water to lunch stop. Lovely prawn and cheese rolls and a tin of beer. Paul got a sore shin. Against my better judgment Reggie's been feeding him bute pills, his answer to 'speed'! Saw Rockingham Castle in the distance as we walked along, up and down the rolling countryside towards Caldecott.

With constant exercise, appetites grew and grew. One evening Mary Holt peeled off to go to a dance in Newmarket. After a couple of hours spent transforming herself from sweaty walker to elegant lady, she found herself drinking champagne on the lawn before at last going in to dinner at nearly 10pm. Some of the tables were decorated with fruit, some with flowers. Hers, by chance, had fruit – and so starving was she by the time the first course arrived she had reduced the centepiece of apples and grapes to a small mound of pips.

Paul Crofts had carried a pair of hair-clippers with him all the way from the start, and every week he had got someone to spruce him up with a Yul Brynner-type haircut. On 5 July, a rest day, Dave Clement's partner Tracy Dawkins came down to join the marchers and borrowed the clippers to give Dave a real low mow. Nathan Oldham arrived on the scene, having just – to his chagrin – spent £5 on a haircut in town. Soon he, too, was bald as a coot. Then the marchers' hostess, Jackie Marriott, decided to have a go at Derek Cross, and eventually the whole gang looked like a bunch of Buddhist monks.

Every morning, about ten minutes after the start, Ed Tate called the office in Gloucestershire on his mobile to say that his team was up and running, and to pick up any news from base. Then in the evening he would go through again to give his contact numbers for that night. But most members of the column felt cut off from the outside world: on the road all day, paralytic with parties in the evening, they had no time to read the newspapers or watch television, and so could not gauge what effect, if any, their marathon effort was having on public opinion.

In fact publicity was very good. The embargo which the organisers had sought to impose had been broken by a whole-page article about the marches in the Weekend Section of the *Daily Telegraph* on 31 May, and that was followed by large spreads in *Sunday* and *Daily Telegraphs* over the weekend of the start from Caldbeck. And yet, in spite of that premature break, media interest in the marches never died away, as Miller Mundy had feared it might.

Tiresome as it was for nominated spokesmen to keep giving interviews to local journalists, morning, noon and night, the cumulative effect was excellent, and, besides the provincial coverage, serious articles about hunting began to appear in the national press. To the organisers' surprise and delight, every one came out against the proposed ban: astonishing as it seemed, no single critical article of any substance appeared during the month in which the marches took place.

The first substantial piece in favour of hunting appeared in the *Independent,* a newspaper from which field-sports enthusiasts would not normally expect much support. Still more encouraging, the author was Polly Toynbee, a journalist renowned for her radical views. In a large article headlined LABOUR SHOULD GO TO EARTH ON FOX-HUNTING, she advised the new government to soft-pedal the issue, and argued that 'only vegetarians have a consistent case for banning hunting,' because 'most farming is horribly cruel.'

Who would not rather be a fox in the wild than a farm animal, let alone a battery hen? A nasty end is better than a nasty life-time. The family picnicking on battery-reared chicken tikka sandwiches is committing greater animal cruelty than the hunt they watch galloping by.

One by one other serious newpapers followed her line, and the march organisers had cause to believe that their crusade was gaining ground. But the men and women trudging southwards could not sense any shift in public opinion, and their days began to seem pretty long. What they did not know was that their courage and dedication were starting to have an important effect elsewhere than in the media. All over Britain country people were gradually becoming aware of the mighty efforts being made on their behalf, not only by the northern army, but by the columns heading in from Wales and Cornwall as well. In the end it was the publicity won by the countryside marches that gave such a boost to the rally in Hyde Park, and lifted the attendance there to a level higher than anyone had dared hope.

CHAPTER FIVE

Out of the West

Down in Cornwall David Latham had been exceedingly active. He had planned his route minutely, using thirteen sheets of the 1:50,000 map, so that in sixteen days' walking, with one rest-day thrown in, the column would cover nearly 300 miles, nominally finishing on the outskirts of London, but in fact at the gates of Ascot racecourse. His aim was to keep off main roads as much as possible, but to pass through several towns so that plenty of people would see the march go by and get its message.

Knowing from his own experience how demoralising it is to find that a day turns out longer than expected – that when you think you are about to finish, you suddenly discover there are still another two miles to go – he had taken the trouble to measure distances precisely with a wheel-gauge, and he planned that every stage should finish not later than 5.30 pm. 'When you're walking like that, it's ideal to have a couple of hours in the evening for a shower and a lie-down before you eat,' he reckons. 'If you don't get in till seven or eight at night, you're too knackered to bother.'

Latham had also recruited many of his thirty-two core walkers, and he asked every one to send him a short *curriculum vitae*, to make sure that nobody had a police record: he did not want any bad eggs on board. Some of the earliest volunteers came forward at the first annual general meeting of the newly-formed East Cornwall Hunt, when the Master, Graham Higgins, spoke about the march. In particular, he sought sponsorship for Sam Taylor, a young man from Bodmin – more heavily tattooed even than Dave Brearley – who lived alone on a small-holding and made his living by going round clipping sheep and doing other odd jobs. Latham, the hunt

Chairman, pointed out that Sam would lose a good deal of money if he walked, and asked people to support him. Hearing the appeal, Brian Webber, a 6'1" beanpole of a farrier, upped and said, 'That's a bloody good idea. I'll drop a tenner in for that.' He put a ten pound note into a cap, and within twenty minutes nearly £400 had been collected – enough for Sam to buy a new pair of boots and send him on his way.

Sitting back in the audience, Webber said to his wife Anita, 'You know, *I* ought to do this. Farriers are so much involved in hunting. I'm buggered if I don't.' Next morning he rang Higgins and said he wanted to go. The response was, 'Are you sure you're fit enough?' When Webber called Latham, the reaction was the same, and his answer was, 'I can soon *get* fit enough.' That did the trick, and he was promptly signed on.

Webber was fifty-nine, and admitted that over the past ten years he had not been in the best of health. Among his troubles were several 'niggling little things,' like having both legs broken by horses. Yet in his teens he had run a marathon, and had done much cross-country endurance training, both as a National Serviceman in the Royal Air Force and afterwards. Now, he felt confident, he could bring himself back to the necessary level of fitness.

The day after the AGM, when he decided to go to London, he went into training. Not being 'a person who'll walk off in a straight line, then turn round and come back,' he worked out a series of loops along country lanes round his farm near St. Austell, and numbered the circuits One to Six. For the first five days he walked No. 1 – a circuit of two and a half miles – once in the morning and once in the evening. Then he began doing No. 1 in the morning and No. 2 (three and a half miles) in the evening, gradually working up until he was covering fifteen miles a day.

Another early volunteer was Amie Pascoe, a dark-haired slip of a farmer's daughter from Philleigh, near Truro. At seventeen, she was waiting to hear how she had fared in her A-levels – and her appearance alone was enough to enliven the march, for she wore rings in both ears, nose and navel. About two weeks after she had signed on, her mother Shirley rang Latham and asked if it would be all right for someone else to join at that late stage.

He answered, 'Yes, if they're fit. Who would it be? Are they fit?' To which, with some embarrassment, Shirley replied, 'I think it'll be me.' In the event she walked tirelessly, almost better than her daughter.

As in the north, training programmes varied widely. For seven weeks before the march began, the beautifully-named June Moon, a forty-eight year old housewife, got up at 5 am and walked ten miles with her lurcher bitch Judy, repeating the hike every evening. Yet even with 500-odd preparatory miles behind her, on the trek itself she suffered from blisters and sore shins. David Daly, the only other blacksmith in the column, trained by walking for three hours after work every evening; Alexander Thavenot, a nineteen-year-old university student, reckoned he was fit anyway, having just returned from three weeks' trekking in Northern Thailand. David Lear, who works for a firm of livestock auctioneers on Exmoor, did no special training, as he signed on only a week before the start-date; but he, too, was fit from previous activity, having completed the London marathon in April and the seventy-mile London-to-Brighton cycle-ride earlier in June.

Latham intended to walk much of the way himself, but because he was also acting as co-odinator for the whole route, and would often be occupied with administrative tasks such as dealing with the press, he wanted to appoint a leader who would regulate the pace every day. One possibility was Mike Brill, a well-known beagler, but for some reason he could not come to the briefing the night before the start. Instead, twenty-four hours before take-off, Latham picked Brian Webber, whose calm demeanour and natural authority marked him out as the obvious choice. Webber's retort was, 'Oh – f – g thanks!' But he took the job on happily enough.

For the briefing, held at 6 pm in the Queen's Hotel at Penzance, Luke Annaly travelled down from Gloucestershire, together with Miller Mundy and Amanda Courtney. Amanda made a brief speech, thanking the core walkers for volunteering, explaining the wider aims of the exercise, and wishing everyone a good journey; but it was Latham who gave them their marching orders. So the stage was set for departure early next morning.

Sunday, 22 June, dawned cool but dry, and by 8 am people were assembling in front of the church at Madron, just outside

Penzance. Core walkers received their yellow T-shirts, spokesmen were assigned to talk to press, radio and television reporters, and just before 9 am Brian Webber called out, 'Right – let's go to London!'

Some people were unfeignedly anxious about what they had taken on. Peter Webb had come all the way from Kent, where he runs a communications business, and his 'complete lack of knowledge about what we were letting ourselves in for' gave him a nervous start. June Moon, also, was apprehensive: she had thought hard before joining, but still could scarcely imagine what lay ahead. Soon, however, people settled down as the column skirted Penzance and headed along the beach. The tide was out, but the splendid, conical hulk of St. Michael's Mount, rising from the sands on their right front, made an unmistakeable landmark: a perfect background for television pictures, and something which advertised to the world that the march was of Cornish origin.

Instead of delegating the lead to others, as Ed Tate had done up north, Brian Webber put himself at the front and stayed there, seeing it as his duty to set a good pace. 'That was the tricky part,' he recalled later, 'finding a pace that all the core could cope with and enjoy. Most of our lads and lasses had done a bit of training, so they had the edge on the day walkers staight off. By the time we'd been going three days, we were all in the swing, and I found if we walked at between three-and-a-half and three and three-quarter miles per hour, that was comfortable. If we tried to go any slower, people found it harder.'

From his service in the RAF Webber had learnt to match strides with more or less anyone, no matter how long or short their legs; and now he found that one of the best core walkers to march with was Alethea Bick, who was only 5'3", but nevertheless fell in easily alongside. His earlier training had also taught him how easily jealousy can spark up if one person is always beside the leader, apparently enjoying his exclusive favours; and so, even though he led, he made sure that he frequently changed companions, and never kept the same man or woman close to him for too long.

The precision of Latham's route planning was evident in his schedule, printed at the top of each day's map:

Sunday 22 June		Grid refs:	
9.00 am	*Depart*	Madron Church	318 453
11.00 am	*Coffee* 4.6 miles	Marazion car park	308 514
1.00 pm	*Lunch* 10.0 miles	Pauls Green Farm, Leedstown	335 599
4.00 pm	*Finish* 18.1 miles	Four Lanes crossroads	386 690

Like Ed Tate in the north, Latham quickly became the object of mild raillery. Whenever he raised his megaphone and gave out a haunting, electronic call, 'Core walkers! Core walkers into single file, please!' the troops would let fly a derisive cheer.

The crusaders soon got an idea of how country people felt about the march. As they passed through a hamlet on the first morning, an old woman, bent with arthritis, stopped Latham and asked what was going on. When he told her, she went into her house and emerged again with a bag of boiled sweets. 'I can't come with you,' she said, 'but take these.'

That first night the party stayed at Scorrier House, near Redruth, magnificent home of the Williams family, who had once been giants in tin-mining. Many of the walkers swam in the pool, and all shared a splendid supper laid on by local people.

Next morning they were off again through the green Cornish countryside: small fields, stone walls and thick hedges – a friendly, intimate landscape. All of them, that is, except Amie Pascoe. News flashed down from London that Mike Foster had agreed to appear on television in face-to-face debate. Since the MP had persistently refused to take part in any discussion of hunting, this was a chance not to be missed. As ambassador for the marches, and the country-side in general, Amanda Courtney selected Amie, who, although barely out of school, was as articulate and determined as anyone.

In a way Amie felt flattered to be chosen, but she was not pleased at having to pull out of that day's march, for she had fully intended to walk every step of the way to London. As it was, her father had to abandon work on the farm for the morning, collect some presentable clothes for her from home, and drive to Truro station, where he bought her tickets. She herself said goodbye to friends in the column and was driven to Truro.

There, she and her father were standing on the platform, and they could see the London express coming in when the tannoy burst into action with the announcement: 'AMIE PASCOE: DO NOT BOARD THE TRAIN.' Was someone pulling her leg? She decided not, and ran back over the bridge, to find a policeman with a message from Amanda, saying that Foster had pulled out of the television programme. Having waited half an hour to get a refund for her unused tickets, she drove off in pursuit of the marchers – and what irritated her most after the event was that Foster gave no reason for backing off.

Her fellow-walkers, when she caught them up in the afternoon, were equally disgusted, and Mark Selway, a freelance journalist, wrote an ironic letter to *Horse and Hound,* suggesting that if Foster found a seventeen-year-old student too intimidating, they could perhaps offer him the youngest member of the column, Michael Alway, aged thirteen. Since this boy – in Selway's estimate – had 'the repartee and scything tongue of a Glaswegian stand-up comedian,' a confrontation might have been fairly entertaining. Unfortunately the magazine did not print Selway's letter.

After that hiccup, a routine was quickly established, similar to that adopted by the northern marchers. The main difference in the West Country was that the Lathams acted as father and mother to the whole party, and so held them together like one large family. David made all the administrative arrangements and dealt with the media, but walked as much as he could each day; Jo drove the back-up van, known as the Yellow Peril, set up drink stops, and held surgeries for people with damaged feet. So vital did her medical work become that she was soon known as the column's ministering angel or Florence Nightingale.

Three times a day, morning, noon and night, she would set out her stall beside the back-up van, deploying a line of folding chairs and little mats for the lame to rest their feet on. Although not a qualified doctor, she had wide medical experience, and it was her combination of skill and sympathy that kept everybody on the road. Her selflessness won everybody's heart. 'That is one special lady,' wrote Martyn Blackmore, a former hunt servant, after the march. 'Nothing was too much trouble for her, even when she was suffering from flu. Every time we stopped she had a hot, smelly foot in her hands, under her nose, and treated it.'

Two of the walkers started out with feet in such bad condition that they were beyond her – she lacked the equipment to tackle in-grown toenails – and she had to send them to a chiropodist. Apart from them, she sorted everybody, dealing with anything from blisters and swellings through sore shins and sprains to ticks and a bite from a Dobermann-Pincher, which rushed out from a new age travellers' site and clamped its jaws into a passing walker's leg.

Her remedy for blisters was to lance them, drain them and cover them with Compeed plasters. Shin problems caused by repetitive jarring were harder to cure. The only real answer was rest, and of course in the circumstances rest was impossible. Instead, 'to give a bit more stability,' she strapped legs up with Animalintex – normally used by vets on horses – and dosed the owners with anti-inflammatory tablets. Towards the end of the march Brian Webber's shins became so bad that she could feel pieces of bone flaking off them, and it was strappings of Animalintex that kept him going. Driving the van at the back of the column, Jo 'made a great study of legs, because I had all day to see how these legs were going.' On the whole it was the men who got into trouble: the nine women and girls in the party went through almost unscathed.

If Derek Cross was the hero of the Coldstream march, the West Country produced its answer in the form of a sea fisherman who does not wish to be identified by any more than his Christian name, Tony. Although he signed on as a core walker, he confided to Latham, a couple of weeks before the start, that he had had a kidney transplant, and was still recovering. Weak though he was, he wanted no sympathy – only to be treated as one of the rest. He said he had been involved in field sports for twenty-five years, since the age of ten, and was determined to walk the full distance.

It was Jo Latham who first realised what deep trouble he was in. He was taking anti-rejection drugs, and the effect of these was to thin his skin. When he got blisters, his feet began to split – not just on the surface, like most people's, but deeper in. When the ball of one foot gaped open, she feared she was not going to be able to keep him on the road.

One night, as she was treating his feet, Jo said to him, 'You're in such a mess, I don't know how you're going to manage tomorrow. I can't give you anything that will even touch the pain you must be going through.'

At that he broke down for a moment, but when she tried to put her arm round him, he threw her off and said loudly, '*I hate my feet!*' Whereupon Jo looked straight at him and said, 'And *I* hate your feet, too!'

Next morning, when he came for treatment, he half-glanced at her and said, 'I hate my feet.'

'So do I,' she answered – and this exchange became their ritual form of greeting.

Brian Webber had not learnt about these problems before the march began, but on the fourth or fifth day Jo called him on the radio to say that Tony was lagging behind, and that his feet were giving him hell. It was only when Webber went to her surgery next morning that he realised how serious the injuries were. Worse followed. Fearing that an infection had started, Jo sent Tony to see a doctor, who prescribed antibiotics; but these clashed with the anti-rejection drugs he was taking and gave him acute diarrhoea. Food began to go straight through him, and on the march he was frequently caught short, having to make a dash for the hedge and sometimes not getting there in time.

Presently he was in such a bad way that, the moment he struggled to the end of a day's stage, he would lie down on the grass and fall asleep. Then, as soon as he had been allocated his overnight accommodation, he would go off, have a bath and put himself straight to bed, without any supper. Naturally he grew weaker and weaker, and there came a day on which Webber seriously considered ordering him home – only to realise that the whole point of the march was to stand up for the rights of individuals. If they were marching for freedom of choice, how could he, the leader, order anyone to do anything? In vain people urged Tony to take half-days off and ride in the van: he refused absolutely, and battled on.

Eventually help arrived in the form of a young woman doctor who came out with the day-walkers. After a talk, she got Tony's medication changed, and, as Webber recalled, 'He put on another face. Next day he could hold on to food, and his strength rallied. But his spirit had never left him – he was so bloody determined.'

Like Dave Clement on the northern march, Peter Webb was keeping a diary. Webb, in his fifties, was not entirely at ease with young people so close to him, and on the third night he found, to his apprehension, that the whole party was to sleep on camp beds in the members' pavilion of the Royal Cornwall Showground at Wadebridge. 'The night was rather rowdy,' he recorded, 'it being the first time we had all slept together':

> Kathryn Bailey, a young point-to-point rider, found my night-shirt rather amusing (Wee Willie Winkie came into it!) At this point I was not sure how to react, but later we got on well. David and Jo were unfortunate in being close to Jeremy Scott-Bolton, who gets very noisy when under the influence, so they did not get much sleep.

Webb wondered if Latham had made the arrangement with some principle in mind – that 'all sleeping in one room contributed to the bonding process thought necessary to get us all to the end of the walk.' In fact the company had been billetted together purely for convenience, and they spent only one other night – the next one – all together. Often things went completely the other way, and one evening Latham had had to split up his thirty-six people between eighteen houses.

In spite of his poor night, Peter Webb found Day Four, from Lanhydrock to Rilla Mills, one of the most attractive and enjoyable parts of the trek, not least because of a memorable lunch laid on by the East Cornwall Hunt:

> We stopped at a barn in a pretty little valley, where locals turned up carrying baskets of food. Tables were laid with home-made Cornish pasties – the best I have tasted – and all manner of salads, sandwiches, cakes, fruit and, best of all, home-made Cornish cream, worth walking a long way for.
>
> After lunch, Sam Taylor had told me, we would be walking by his farm. Standing out on a hillside, the white farmhouse looked very pretty, with the land disappearing behind a hill. Later we passed some of his sheep quietly waiting for his return in over two weeks' time.

Cornish pasties became such a feature of the march that Martyn Blackmore invented a new name for them: rat coffins. Later that afternoon the column crossed Bodmin Moor, and a former MFH explained to Webb how difficult it was to ride over the low-growing gorse. The horses did not like it, he said: they tried to jump from one grassy patch to the next, and as it was impossible to tell which way a horse would go next, some nasty falls resulted.

Next morning – Day Five – members of the East Cornwall Hunt escorted their guests to the border with Devon, the bridge over the Tamar at Horsebridge. 'And sad were we to leave them,' wrote Webb. 'We felt rather like the Hobbit when it entered the land of Mordor, for on crossing the bridge we had no time to take pictures of this most picturesque spot, but were whisked past the pub, where the hospitable landlord had coffee on the boil.'

The entry into Tavistock gave everyone a powerful lift. Until then they had been rather disappointed with the numbers turning out to wish them well. Admittedly the population of Cornwall is sparse – but even so, there was a feeling that people could have made more effort. Now for the first time they became aware of what deep feelings they could stir up in the local population: at least 500 people turned out to march with them through the town.

With Tavistock behind them, they toiled on up the steep ascent on to Dartmoor. Rain had been threatening all day, and now the drizzle turned into a downpour, driven horizontally by an icy wind. The combination produced a high wind-chill factor, especially dangerous to the marchers who had heated up during the climb. Soon two of them began to deteriorate: if they did not find shelter quickly, they would be in serious trouble.

Through the flying rain they spotted two buildings ahead, one a large pub, the other a white cottage. The landlord of the inn had already given offence by telling David Latham that nobody might use his lavatories without paying; so they went straight past and descended on the cottage. The reaction of the owners, Nigel and Janet Knight, was magnificent. Somehow they crammed all thirty-five of the party into their tiny kitchen and thawed them out, plying them with cups of tea and home-made cakes while rainwater dripped down off sodden clothes to flood the flagstone floor. Their wonderful, spontaneous hospitality was something the marchers could never forget.

That night, however, brought a sharp let-down. Their host had not only invited the party to stay: he had positively insisted that they should all sleep in his large house. But when they reached it, still wet and cold, they found to their chagrin that they were not welcome indoors. One woman described indignantly how they walked inside, and the owner 'started shoutin' and hollerin' "What are you lot doing? You do as you're told"' – whereupon he ordered them out into the stable. When they found they had to sleep in a loft which was being renovated, with the wind whistling though, there was almost a mutiny. Latham himself was shocked by the conditions, but simply had to ask everyone to accept what was on offer. People drew savage amusement from the slogan on the back of their host's horsebox: IT'S A GREAT DAY – WATCH SOME BASTARD SPOIL IT.

Next day was a rest day, and the walkers went back into Tavistock to explore the town. They met one small rebuff, when a woman in a bicycle shop refused to sell a waterproof cape because she disapproved of hunting, but otherwise their reception was as cordial as could be.

That single bad night apart, the hospitality offered to the travellers was phenomenal. Some of them were slightly overawed by the grandeur of the houses in which they stayed, but all were full of praise and gratitude for the generosity shown them. The sentence 'We were treated like kings and queens' crops up in one report after another. One highlight, for many, was Cotley Place, home of the Eames family, who have owned the Cotley Harriers, with their white hounds, for 200 years. The whole of the huge Victorian house was a mass of hunting history. Another evening, fifteen-year-old James Sealy was particularly impressed when, within twenty minutes of him reaching his billet, 'hosts went out and left us keys to house and Land Rover, food in freezer and drink in fridge.'

Ridiculous incidents occurred – as when June Moon was put to stay with people called Bennett, along with eight other ladies. 'They had one of these baths that you press a button, and all air bubbles come up,' recalled June in her soft Cornish burr. 'Of course I'd never seen anything like that before. I put some Radox B bathsalts in, and walked out to get a hot drink.' When she came back, not just the bath, but the whole room, was a mass of foam. 'I shouted "HELP!" and one of the sons come running in. I flyed in the bath, and all you could see was my face.' With much hilarity and shrieking, the other women took turns in the bath, and many photos were shot of nymphs disporting themselves in the foam mountain.

At the start of the march some Cornishmen and women felt a little sad that they were leaving home and heading into the unknown: the farther they went, the less familiar their surroundings became, the fewer the day-walkers whom they recognised. Yet one man, at least, had the opposite sensation. David Lear, the auctioneer, had lived on Exmoor for the past twelve years and, as he moved eastwards, felt he was going home.

His main reason for joining the march was his knowledge of farming on Exmoor, and his appreciation of the contribution that hunting makes to the area. With stag-hunting already banned on National Trust land, he knew that many people's jobs and way of life were threatened, and that if further curbs were imposed on field sports, the economy of the whole region would be undermined: hotels, shops, petrol stations, farmers' wives doing bed and break-fast – all would suffer. 'Is it a coincidence that the finest herds of red deer in the land are to be found in those areas hunted by the three packs of West Country stag-hounds?' he asked; and in interviews with the media he lost no opportunity of stressing how different life on Exmoor would be if the Government 'passed laws which would not in fact save the life of a single animal, but would undoubtedly bring about less humane deaths among our wildlife.'

Far from clashing with critics along the way, he was buoyed up by 'overwhelming levels of support.' In all seventeen days of the march, 'you could count those who didn't support us on the fingers of two hands,' and the commitment of local people to the cause seemed so strong that 'it was difficult to imagine that anyone would *not* be in Hyde Park on 10 July.'

On Day Nine – the one when the party reached Cotley – Peter Webb had intended to go home and return to work in Kent. In the event he found it impossible to desert all the new friends he had made. 'These were honest people, many of whom would lose their jobs if they failed,' he wrote. 'I did not want to diminish the cause by deserting in the middle.' By then his feet were hurting severely: they had grown, or swollen, to at least one size bigger than normal, and he was obliged to take a lift into Chard, where he bought a pair of expensive Nike Air trainers. But he knew that many fellow marchers were suffering even more, from blisters, twisted ankles, sore shins and swollen knees: many were bandaged and downing pain-killers by the handful, or holding ice-cubes on their shins to dull the persistent ache – and this made him all the more determined to carry on. As if further proof of sheer guts were needed, it came that afternoon, when Nick Bryant and Dave Aubin, who had been obliged to start three hours behind the main party that morning, walked straight through the day, without a break, moving so fast that they reached their destination only one hour behind the main bunch.

Several of the group did not much care for the way they were expected to promote their cause by carrying placards, with slogans like 'THIS IS REAL LIFE, NOT THE ARCHERS' and 'COUNTRY SPORTS MEAN COUNTRY BUSINESS.' They felt that such direct messages turned the march into too much of a demonstration, and once, as Webb put it, they stowed some of the placards in the back-up van 'to make the effect less intimidating.' He himself found the task of carrying a placard 'quite embarrassing. At first I tried to hide behind it, but as time went on I got more used to the idea, and was able to look passers-by in the face without blushing.'

Another exacting job was that of handing out Code of Conduct cards to anyone in reach. The cards gave a brief outline of the purpose of the marches – 'a response to the frustration and concern felt by country people against the threats posed to the countryside and their jobs by politicians and urban influence, through pre-judice, ignorance and diminishing rural representation.' There was also a call for support, and a section which could be torn off and sent to the Marches Office, with the name and address of a backer filled in.

Peter Webb found that the task of distribution 'required extra reserves of strength, which were beyond me, as it was necessary to depart from the route to give the cards to the motorist or passer-by, by which time the marchers had moved on, and you had to run to catch up.' Several people, however, had the energy to do this continually, among them Mike Brill, Dave Aubin and Luke Annaly, who had joined the column at Shaftesbury and walked the rest of the way.

On they went, from Devon into Dorset, through Dorset into Hampshire, with the weather heating up all the way, and morale rising steadily as the level of support increased. After the ferocious climb into the centre of Shaftesbury, they were revived by the chance remark of an old lady who asked Simon Copperwait where they had come from.

'Cornwall,' was the answer.

'Goodness! she exclaimed. 'You must have started very early!'

Not much news of the other columns had filtered through, and Mark Selway, the journalist, was eager to know how their competitors were faring: 'Rumour abounded: the Scots were receiving the most brilliant support as they flew down the country. Worse still, they were drinking more than us. We heard that the Welsh, who had started after us, were covering more ground per day, with marches of over thirty miles. We would have loved to have known what they heard of us.' Normally working on his own, Selway was struck by strength of team feeling that developed, and reckoned he had never known such cameraderie since leaving the army.

From Salisbury the column struck out across country along the Clarendon Way, an ancient track dating from the twelfth century, when it was made to give easy access to Clarendon Park, Henry II's hunting lodge. Having walked up on to the downs, the marchers passed the site of the lodge in the woods, but saw no sign of a building. After so many miles of smooth tarmac, the uneven, rutted surface of the track demanded greater concentration, and meant that people walked with their heads down, missing most of the lovely, rolling landscape, golden with ripening corn. A grand welcome awaited them at Stockbridge, where the local community, though given more to shooting and fishing than to hunting, turned out in force. The only person disappointed was young Xan

71

Thavenot, a mustard-keen fisherman who thought he had arrived
in heaven when he reached the Test, only to find that somebody
else had been billeted on the house which had fishing on the river.

Next morning, with three days to go, Tony, who had been so ill,
told Brian Webber that he was fed up with bringing up the rear of
column: could he come up the front for a while? Webber of course
agreed, and from that point the two walked side by side; but all the
while Webber was hatching a secret plot whereby, right at the end,
he would hand over the Cornish flag, which he himself had been
carrying much of the way, and give Tony the honour of bearing it
across the finishing line, 'as my thankyou to a very brave Cornish-
man.' When friends told him Tony would never do it, Webber
replied, 'You want to bet? I bet he bloody does!'

As they led the column up Ascot High Street, Webber was
carrying the flag in his left hand. Looking back, as if in doubt,
he said to his companion, 'Slow down a bit, Tony. We're going too
fast. The day-walkers are getting strung out.' Next he started to
walk backwards, pretending to check the ranks behind; then he
casually transferred the flag from left hand to right and said, 'Here,
Tony, hold this a minute for me.' So Tony took the flag. Webber
stepped away from him, and without realising what he was doing,
the hero carried the flag over the line. As he passed between the
gateposts on to the race-course, a roar of applause burst from the
spectators. Suddenly everyone was whooping and cheering and
hugging each other, overcome by emotion. Tony turned towards
his leader and said, 'You bastard!'

CHAPTER SIX

The Dragon Awakes

In Central and North Wales David Jones had recruited many of his core marchers by the simple expedient of ringing up friends and telling them they had better walk to London. If any hesitated, he assured them that beyond Kington, in Herefordshire, the road was downhill all the way . . . His personal magnetism played an important part in collecting the team; and it also ensured that he had a nucleus of people whom he knew and could trust absolutely not to let him down: 'I wanted people who wouldn't get into difficulties along the way, because they'd know how to behave themselves.'

One volunteer/victim was young Ian Hawkins from Brecon:

'David phoned and said, "Are you coming to London with me?" 'I said, "Who's going?" 'He said, "There's you and me and Roy Savage so far."

'I thought, Oh – he's joking. But he wasn't.'

By such means Jones assembled thirty-two core walkers. Faced with the prospect of taking that many people on a long journey, he felt the group must have some money for immediate expenses, and some in reserve. In England there were plenty of well-to-do folk in large houses who would put the marchers up, but the beginning of the route ran through the countries of relatively modest hunts, without the premises or the means to lay on large-scale entertainment; and the organisers decided that their best plan would be to give everyone an evening meal in a pub, after which locals could return to their own homes by car, giving beds to those from farther afield. Later, if they ever fell short of accommodation, they would have the funds to book a few of their people into a hotel for a night.

The core walkers therefore sought local sponsorship, and raised several thousand pounds.

As on the other marches, the company included people of every description. Stephen Robbins, an eighteen-year-old student, had just taken his A-levels and booked a holiday in Ibiza along with twenty friends. At the last moment he decided to sell his place on the trip and march instead. Sue Morgan, a post lady from Knighton, cancelled a holiday in Spain so that she could take part. She was used to walking seven miles a day on her round, but for a month before take-off she put in another six or eight miles' training on five or six nights a week. Anna Turner, a wife, mother and part-time book-keeper from Shropshire, biked for ten miles and walked for two hours on alternate days, and also swam get fit, because she objected 'to being told by ill-informed politicians, who have listened to a few strident voices, how life in the countryside should be conducted.' Gail Greenhouse, who decorates figurines, also believed that country people should manage their own environment: she had trained by running three miles a day and walking from ten to fifteen miles at weekends.

Several people joined by degrees, as it were, setting off with the idea that they would show solidarity by marching for a couple of days, but in fact staying the whole course. One such was Austin James, Huntsman of the Albrighton and Woodland in Warwickshire, but originally from Carmarthenshire. Some years earlier he and his partner Karen Turner had both been injured by a car that swept up from behind when they were exercising hounds at 5.40 am and knocked them both flying. Karen had fully recovered, and had signed on as a core marcher, but Austin was still wearing two corsets to support damaged discs, and thought that one stint on the road would be all he would manage. Yet after Day One his back seemed none the worse, so he did Day Two, and Day Three . . . and just kept going.

Another of the same ilk was Roger Hughes, a dairy and sheep farmer who does not hunt or fish or shoot, but nevertheless supports the David Davies hounds by walking puppies every summer – something his family has done for three generations at least. A year before, he had completed the Cross-Wales Walk – a forty-five mile marathon, done in a single day, which raises money for charity; and in spite of the fact that the effort had left him 'completely jiggered', he was planning to go in for the event again. Then it was cancelled because the weather had become so atrocious, and he felt he should walk *somewhere* to justify the sponsorship money which he had raised. Thus, when David Jones asked him, 'Are you coming to London?' Hughes agreed to go for the first two or three legs . . . only to find himself hooked, eventually, by the extraordinary feelings of kinship which the communal endeavour of the trek created.

On the morning of 27 June the march went off to a cracking start, with 222 men and women in the column. Many of the core marchers were apprehensive, not least Heather Tylor, forty-seven years old, artist, mother and Joint Master of the Bicester with Whaddon Chase. 'Woke up around 5 am, horribly nervous, full of self-doubt, wondering what on earth had possessed me to think I could do this walk,' she recorded in her diary.

As the marchers geared themselves up for take-off, the Mayor of Machynlleth wished them well in a brief address from the base of the tower. A banner appeared bearing the words DROS RYDDID COLLASANT EIN GWAED (FOR FREEDOM WE SHED OUR BLOOD) – a quotation from the Welsh National Anthem. Somebody launched into the anthem itself, *Hen Wlad fy Nhadau* - Land of my Fathers – which was sung with such fervour that many people were moved to tears. Then, on the stroke of nine, away they went.

After the kite-haunted passage across the golf course, described on Page One, the first leg was tough by any standards: a steep climb out of Machynlleth, and on over the hills for twenty-seven miles. Jones was under no illusion as to the severity of the route, because he and a friend, Huw Thomas, had reconnoitred it together, each walking half the distance. Yet he knew that in the empty hills of Central Wales they had no alternative: there was no good stopping place short of Llanidloes.

Thomas was another core walker. Having sold his dairy processing and wholesaling business a few years earlier, he had time both to train and to march. For two weeks before the start he had been out in the hills every other day for four hours at a stretch.

Now, on Day One, as the marchers went past the broadcaster Wynford Vaughan Thomas's memorial – a circular turret looking towards Cader Idris – locals felt sorry for the strangers in the company, because under a heavy sky the scenery was not showing to best advantage. But then as they came down towards the great dam at Clywedog the weather brightened and the views became magnificent. English walkers were disconcerted to see guard dogs patrolling on the dam: nothing to do with the march, but a reminder of the fact that in those wild hills there lurk extremists who would dearly love to blow up the system that supplies water to Birmingham and other English cities.

As the marchers settled down and grew used to each others' company, characters quickly emerged – and none was easier to identify than Austin James, whose cackle of laughter sent everyone into paroxysms. There was no need to hear the remark that had set Austin the Laugh off: the mere sound of him starting up was enough to throw anyone near him into fits. Often his foil was Richard Williams, a small, dark, neat-featured farmer from Snowdonia with an inexhaustible propensity for cracking jokes: whenever those two got going, the whole column became convulsed.

Never mind that this was difficult farming country, with poor soil and high rainfall. From the start the level of hospitality was overwhelming. The column's first lunch stop, in Donald Meddins's barn, struck David Jones as being 'like the Last Supper, there was that much food there.' Again, when they made an unscheduled stop in a farmyard, the youngsters went in first, looking for a drink of water. As soon as the lady of the house heard what they were doing, she brought out bottles of squash, and her daughter quickly made a whole tray-full of sandwiches.

After her nervous start, Heather Tylor soon settled down:

The first twenty miles slipped by happily among the beautiful Welsh hills. David Jones came and passed a few miles with me. He is a most charming man; I am beginning to see why he is held in such esteem and why he is such an ambassador for our sport. I hope he is strong enough to control his little army if we encounter any opposition along the way.

I am pleased with the way I can keep walking. The last five miles are hard – legs really ache – but amazingly I am no worse off than any of the others after twenty-seven miles as fast as we can go. No blisters, no injuries: I am very lucky. Drink two pints of lager straight off on hitting the pub. This amuses the lads, and I am established as a two-pint man from now on. Excellent dinner, very tired: hot bath and early bed extremely welcome. Sleep impossible because the legs ache, because of the peacock and because of the fear of not making it tomorrow.

For Tom Barrow, a land agent from High Wycombe, the highlight of the first day (apart from the kite) was seeing a fisherman catch a brown trout in a lake beside the path – an event hailed 'with a large cheer from us all.' Hughes, also, enjoyed the day, hard as it was, and decided to do another.

Again the morning was drizzly, and mist spoilt the view as the marchers looked down from the heights on to the ruins of the monastic settlement of Abbeycwmhir. All the same, most of them were excited by the grandeur of the walk over the hills to Penybont. That was another long stint – twenty-three miles – and in the opinion of Tony Hinde, a free-lance photographer from Shropshire, 'the planners had a brilliant knack of giving us a steep hill to climb at the start of every day, and another at the finish.' Heather Tylor was irritated by the way young Charles Frampton insisted on 'running along in front' so that he could reach the pub in Penybont in time to watch the Lions' second rugby test against South Africa on Sky television.

'As it turned out,' Hinde reported, 'the place had no satellite TV. But a couple of the lads had Walkman radios, with earphones, and as we panted up the hill into the village, a cheer rose from the top and the message came back down, "The Lions have scored a penalty!" ' In the pub, they all crowded round a transistor radio to listen to the second half of the match. Pip Jones felt that 'it was like going back about thirty years, when everybody used to get round the radio to listen to the boxing matches.' When Jeremy Guscott dropped a goal, to settle the series, the place erupted. Hughes was delighted to find a 1950s poster advertising the trotting races, which still take place in Penybont every year. The bottom line promised that 'the Show Dance will be in the Iron Room' – a fine period description of a corrugated-tin shack. Then, without warning, a radiator fell off the wall: Austin the Laugh let fly one of his hyena cackles, and sent everyone into hysterics. Anticipation rose sharply when word went round that thirty Swedish girls were on holiday at a nearby trekking centre, but excitement was quickly doused by the news that the owner was not keen to make introductions.

Heather found the final stage tough going: 'The last hill really hurts, and we are all shattered at the end.' But she enjoyed the evening in the pub: 'Great fun watching everyone try to get up from the table and walk to the bar: we are all so stiff, just getting back on to our feet is a real problem.'

As the company shaped up for Day Three, Hughes had half-decided to carry on the whole way. He felt that 'It was too good an opportunity to miss, for every reason.' Before he could organise any remaining objections in his mind, David Jones started giving the morning's instructions and handing out a few extra core walkers' yellow T-shirts. 'One went to Austin James,' Hughes recalls, 'and the other came flying in my direction. It was "Catch this!" and I was on my way to London.'

His immediate reward was a glorious day's walk over Radnor Forest and down to the Herefordshire market town of Kington. Skylarks were singing, and the column of brightly-clad marchers, with the red-dragon banner at its head, made a stirring spectacle as it wound over the rounded green hills. 'David Morgan has become our self-appointed field master in order to tone down the pace,' Heather reported:

Heaven help anyone who steps in front of him. Under his little green woollen hat and rather benign, dwarfish appearance, he's extremely ferocious. A most popular and endearing member of the team, so long as we know our place behind him. Charles Frampton is given the radio to carry at the back as a penance for his previous misdemeanours at the front, so things settle down to a sensible pace.

It was not only Heather who had been finding the pace too hot. Most people had been complaining, and at one point on the third day a despairing cry came up from the back: 'Tell them to slow down. I've just run over a rabbit.'

Day Four brought the party out of the hills and through lush Herefordshire farm land. For Hughes the highlight was the lunch stop at a lovely old black-and-white mill on the River Arrow, where he sat on the weir by an eel-trap and thought how he would love to live beside water. To him, the place was idyllic, the heart of the countryside – what the whole march was about.

That morning David Jones had nearly lost his voice. Was it from singing? someone asked him. 'No,' he said. 'It was just that in the pub last night I laughed till I was hoarse.'

To walk beside the leader was to gain deep insights into the way hunting permeates life in the Welsh countryside. Hounds have existed in Wales for more than a thousand years, he said: 'In the ninth century AD the legendary Hywel Dda – Hywel the Good – had a pack of hunting dogs with all the characteristics of the Welsh foxhound of today.' There are now more than 500 packs in the principality, some 230 of them gun-packs: in country too steep and rough for horses, essential fox-control is carried out by half a dozen hounds and a large number of foot-followers armed with shotguns.

Jones himself was born in a council house in Merthyr Tydfil, at the head of the mining valleys in South Wales. His father, a plumber, was a keen fisherman and shot, but never hunted. Yet somehow hunting was in the boy's blood, and he began when he was fourteen, taken up by his father to ride with the Sennybridge Farmers' Hounds on the northern slopes of the Brecon Beacons. In 1967, at the age of twenty-four he formed his own pack, the Taf Fechan, at Merthyr – and got 'an amazing response.' Before that, there had been no hounds in Merthyr for quarter of a century, and their return created a minor sensation: on Boxing Day the hunt would meet outside the Town Hall, at the express request of the Mayor and Council.

After six seasons there, Jones moved to his present post with the David Davies hounds, which he has now hunted for twenty-four seasons, one day a week on horseback, two days on foot. Listen to him talk about his job:

The most foxes we've ever killed in a season was 200. This season gone we got 156. A lot of the time we're out in response to lambing calls. This time one farmer, David Richards, lost thirty-

79

seven lambs. Another woman lost twenty-two in a week, and the neighbouring farm twelve in three nights.

Now if anyone tells you foxes don't take live lambs, he's got another think coming to him. If Mike Foster came to Wales, I could collect him in Rhayader and drive him up the A 470 and tell him to pick any farm he liked. We could go there, and I could guarantee him that the farmer would have had problems with foxes.

Once you get a rogue fox, you've got serious problems. The odd thing is that he'll travel a long way to kill in a particular area, so he takes some finding. When we answer a lambing call, we go in the early morning, because with the dew down, the scent holds. Our hounds are deeper-scented, so they'll pick up the drag of a night line. The fox may have gone two or three hours earlier, but in the end they'll put him up, and you know you've got the one that's doing the damage.

The sad thing is that none of these politicians are the least bit interested *in the fox*. He's thrived for all these years *because of* hunting. If they take hunting away, he'll pretty well disappear. He'll be cut in numbers so vastly that nobody will ever see him.

It was the sheer ignorance of politicians that caused most anger among the marchers. 'We're being pressured by an urban majority who know absolutely nothing about us,' said Richard Williams, Austin the Laugh's joking partner. Williams is Master of the Eryri Hounds (the name, a version of 'eyrie', means 'Home of the Eagle'), whose kennels are at the foot of Snowdon, and knows those wild mountains as well an any man. 'Townspeople are very well-meaning, I daresay, but they do not know what they're talking about. They try to accuse us of cruelty. My family have farmed at Snowdon for 400 years. If we'd been cruel to our animals, we'd never have survived in the business for this long.'

Field sports were by no means the only area in which the Welsh felt threatened. With village schools and cottage hospitals closing, bus services running down and railways defunct, they perceived that the Government neither knew nor cared what life was like out in the wilds. Politicians had no inkling of the way in which the hunt and the football club are often the only institutions which still bind small communities together. It was symptomatic of the huge gap between town and country that of the fifty people going by coach to the rally from Huw Thomas's village, Caersws, twenty had never before been to London.

The basic issue at stake – several people said – was that of personal freedom. 'You want to know why I'm walking?' asked one farmer sharply. 'My father fought a world war for freedom of choice. That's why.' From up and down the column there came mutters about resorting to civil disobedience if the Government did not see sense. 'Welshmen are fiery devils anyway,' said one man. 'The feeling's that high: they're already talking about burning forestry, blocking roads, blowing up water-pipes. You're going to see problems, I can tell you. It's too late. Michael Foster's done it. He's put the bill up. He'll be responsible for an awful lot of things that are going to happen. If they carry on as they are, they'll turn this country into another Ulster.'

Serious though the marchers' cause might be, they were in high spirits for most of the time – and never more so than one evening at supper in a pub. In Stephen Robbins's memory 'the dining room was a mass of yellow T-shirts. We knew that a TV debate about hunting had been going on, and suddenly David Jones stopped the buzz of chatter to tell us the result: sixty-two per cent of the people who had rung in were NOT in favour of a ban. The pub windows were nearly shattered by the roar of approval, mixed in with several spine-tingling hollers.'

Another night Robbins found himself sharing a room with 'a well-known MFH from a pack in North Wales,' and woke in the night to hear his companion mutter in his sleep, 'Why don't you shut up and listen for a minute, you silly fucker?'. In the morning, when Robbins asked the MFH who he thought he might have been talking to, the answer was, 'It is very likely to have been Mr Foster.'

The farther the march progressed, the more the walkers came to venerate their support driver, Pip Jones from Newtown, whose beaming smile and unnshakeable good humour kept them going day after day. A former civil engineer, with his own business, Pip could not himself walk far because he had had major operations on his spine; but he had done a good deal of back-up work on long-distance hikes, so he volunteered again, and found himself 'driving the Blister Bus from Machynlleth to London.' The orange Transit box-van, also known as the Tango Van, became the marchers' essential comfort station. Not only did it transport their haversacks and day-bags from start to finish: out of the back of it Pip dispensed water, squash, blister packs, pain-killers, and above all, bananas.

The appetite for bananas was insatiable: the column put away 4,500 during the course of their journey. One morning, when asked by one of the boys for pain-killers, Pip produced some tablets, but as he read the instructions on the packet, he exclaimed, 'Hang on. It says that these must only be taken with food, at meal-times.' Then quick as a flash he added, 'Have a banana!' Pip had no formal medical training, but he had practised a good deal on his wife's feet and those of her companions on their long-distance walks. His patent method of dealing with a blister was to push a needle and thread through and leave the cotton overnight, so that it would drain off the fluid. The kit for the van had been admirably planned by the marches office, but the demand for medical supplies proved so strong that the back-up team kept having to resort to chemists along the way. 'Every day we were going through about £50 worth, if we could get hold of it,' Pip recalled. 'Compeed heel blisters cost about £3 apiece, and some days we were using ten boxes. We went into the chemists' in Ledbury and cleaned them out.' He also got through colossal quantities of what he called 'anaesthetic' – to ordinary mortals, gin. For the worst sufferers, G-and-T became the best pain-killer of all.

From the van also came an endless supply of white T-shirts bearing the black logo of the countryside march. These were sold to all-comers at £5 apiece, and earned a healthy profit for the central march fund. Pip's van alone shifted 1,500. 'They were all the same size,' Pip admitted, 'but we told everyone not to worry about that. Whoever it was, they'd fit!'

By the end of Day Four Heather was feeling the strain:

> The last hours seemed endless and very painful. Austin James walked with me at the end. His hurried little stride, accompanied by the twang of metal from his stick on the road, always heralded his arrival from behind. His constant good humour just got me through the day, dead tired, wet through, everything hurting.

Luckily Day Five was a rest day, and Day Six an agreeable, relatively gentle advance south-eastwards through the rolling Herefordshire hills, with a lunch-stop at the Trumpet Inn, on the Ledbury road. There the column was rejuvenated by the addition of sixty boys and girls, together with several of the teaching staff, from The Elms preparatory school at Colwall, near Malvern. The headmaster, Clive Ashby, had given a talk on country sports, putting the pros and cons, and asked pupils if they would like to join the march. Sixty volunteers were ferried the short distance to the start in mini-buses. The children, in their claret-coloured sweaters, walked all that afternoon to the finish at Eastnor Castle, the vast, mock-Gothic fortress belonging to the Hervey-Bathurst family.

Half a mile short of the castle, word came that for once the antis had mobilised a protest force, so the marchers brought the children into the middle of the column, to make sure they were not scared, and instructions went out that everyone was to walk straight past any demonstrators, ignoring them. Even so, as Heather described it, the sight of twenty scruffy but vociferous 'hippy-looking types produced an instantaneous response from our gang, who gave tongue with excitement. For one minute I feared the worst, until David Jones restored order and steered us over the drawbridge into the castle.'

That evening the Elms contingent went back to base, while the marchers feasted splendidly, guests of the Hervey-Bathursts. In the morning the children rejoined, fresh as paint, but Heather was plagued by her usual problems:

Wake up early, adrenaline running, still afraid I won't get there, still afraid the legs won't hold up. Get up early, get them working, get rid of some of the stiffness. Check boots and socks are dry. Make the only vital decisions of the day: Boots or trainers? Stick or no stick?

Before leaving Eastnor, David Jones gave a stern lecture about keeping the march peaceful. He also had to silence a faction who were all for diverting northwards to Worcester and visiting their friend Mr Foster in his constituency.

Even without diversions that day – Day Seven – proved easily the most aggravating of the entire journey. The route was from Eastnor, up over the southern tongue of the Malvern hills, down across the Severn Vale and over Bredon Hill to the Gloucestershire village of Ashton-under-Hill. For once the organisers had made a serious miscalculation: the day was officially listed as a short one, and the length of the leg given as eighteen miles; but, according to one infuriated marcher who measured the distance with a ped-ometer, the column covered thirty-two miles before they slithered to the finish, soaked and exhausted. According to the schedule, they should have reached the end between 4.30 and 5 pm: in fact the last of them came in after 7.30. The most frustrating aspect of the marathon was that for hours they could see the 'bloody great hill' of Bredon in the distance ahead: they knew they would have to climb it towards the end of the day, yet as they tacked back and forth, north and south, it never seemed to come any closer. The children from The Elms walked as far as the stop for elevenses, then fell out and returned to school. After a long morning, the marchers reached Upton-on-Severn, where a piper met them, then led them the through the town and over the Severn bridge, to lunch laid on in a marquee by the river. According to Tom Barrow, 'Some of the locals cheered, and others must have felt we were a Welsh army on the way to London.'

On again, still meandering rather than going straight forward, they had to manoeuvre round or over one obstacle after another: a canal, a major sewage works, the M5, the River Avon. At least, as they crossed the motorway, lorry drivers speeding below hooted and waved encouragement, thus boosting morale. But still Bredon Hill rose in front of them on the eastern horizon.

One or two people remembered that Bredon was the model for Brensham Hill, immortalised in John Moore's classic autobiogra-phical memoir *Brensham Village*. Those who knew the book consoled themselves by remembering some of the eccentric char-acters whom Moore depicted, from the terminally-impoverished Mad Lord, to the hermit who lived on rabbits which he caught with his hands and ate raw, and the shameless rector, Mr Mountjoy, who allowed poachers to promenade the hill with him. (Every now and then one of them would dodge into the bushes to set a snare, but whenever a gamekeeper accosted them and demanded to know what they were doing, the answer was always, 'A-walkin' with his Reverence.')

One man who did know every inch of the ground was Steven Hill, a lorry driver and labourer, who was brought up in Pensham, a village just north of Bredon Hill. As a boy he was constantly up and down the steep slopes, and now, 'by a million-to-one chance', he had the opportunity of walking to the very spot on which the family had scattered his father's ashes.

Most of the marchers, however, had never heard of Bredon, or Moore, or Brensham, and were preoccupied with their own problems. By the time they reached the base of the hill, Richard Williams was in a really bad way with his splintering shin: even liberal doses of his patent remedy, gin-and-tonic, did little to dull the pain, and he had fallen well behind, hobbling along on crutches. After the column had crossed the canal and paused for tea, with sumptuous cakes, David Jones told him, 'For heaven's sake stop torturing yourself and take a ride in the van.' But he refused, and struggled on.

'We almost had to carry Richard up Bredon Hill,' reported Heather. 'He is in desperate pain, but never stops telling jokes in his wonderful deep voice. His talent to amuse never deserts him.' While a posse of supporters escorted him, others pressed on, Roger Hughes reckoning that 'when you come to a hill, everybody seems to jump up a cog and go that much quicker.' Half-way over, the leaders met Sam Butler, walking out to meet them from the opposite end. Steady rain set in and turned the slope into a mud-slide. Four or five of the men at the front started running, only half in control. 'I was running with them,' Hughes remembered. 'I jumped over this gate and went flying down this bank, arrived covered in mud top to bottom.'

Pip Jones, driving on ahead, had already discovered to his disgust that the route ended at a derelict barn, which looked as though it had been unoccupied for years, with stinging nettles head-high in the doorway and a sloping sheet of mud on the approach outside. 'There was nowhere for anyone to sit down, nowhere for anyone to get dry. We were still miles from anywhere. It was a crazy, crazy place.'

Far behind the leaders, Williams and his party were still struggling on. Mark Allen, the man driving the back-up vehicle, kept apologising about the distance, and at 6.35 pm he assured them they would be in within fifteen minutes. Forty-five minutes later, they were still limping downhill towards the barn.

The miseries of the day dissolved in a warm sea of hospitality. Geoff Bow was picked up by a farmer, along with a couple of others, and driven home. 'As we came in through the door, the farmer's wife said, "You'd better pull your clothes off and get them washed." So we did, and jumped into the bath. When we came down to the kitchen she looked out of the window, saw it was still raining, and said, "Now you'd better go in the tumble drier." The farmer said, "Here's a bottle of Scotch for you, and one for me. That way, we can't fall out." '

Tom Barrow and others were picked up the Beldam family of Stanton Broadway, who ferried them back 'to a hot bath, full laundry service, a hefty vodka-and-tonic, and dinner. Mrs Beldam then attended to blisters with a needle and thread (no screams heard).' Then and later the level of hospitality continued to be almost overwhelming. Steven Hill summed it up by saying, 'I live in a caravan, and you could have got it into most of the bathrooms where I stayed!' On the whole the guests behaved themselves with decorum, although now and then somebody over indulged. After a mass invasion in a place that had better remain nameless, the host was constrained to remark, 'Only one of them missed the lavatory.'

As the men and women from Machynlleth forged across Central Wales, another column was heading eastwards from its start-point at St. Clears, far out in Carmarthenshire. The South Wales march was largely the creation of two men, Adrian Simpson, Regional Director of the BFSS for Mid Wales, and Simon Hart, Sam Butler's brother-in-law and Master of the South Pembrokeshire Hunt. Spurred on by fears that little publicity might be won in the empty heartlands of Mid Wales, they conceived the idea of a supplementary trek closer to centres of population in the south, and in particular within easy reach of Cardiff, home of the *Western Mail* and *South Wales Echo*, BBC Radio Wales, S4C television, HTV, and the Red Dragon commercial radio station.

At first BFSS head office was not keen that one of its own regional staff should become involved in the marches: as has been shown, in the early stages of planning the Society viewed them with some suspicion. Nevertheless, the two organisers pressed ahead with arrangements, helped by Sam Butler, who twice travelled down for meetings in Carmarthen. The original idea was that both Welsh marches should walk to a meeting point – perhaps Malvern – but it was found that logistic problems made this impossible, and in the end the southern management settled on a compromise: their team would walk for six days, across the heads of the old mining valleys, then up to Abergavenny and Monmouth, whence they would be lifted by bus to join the Machynlleth column at Ashton-under-Hill.

The organisers thought that if they could attract a dozen core walkers, that would be enough. In fact word-of-mouth soon lined up over twenty, and two or three more joined by degrees, as in the north. In Hart's words, 'Once they'd got a taste for it, they couldn't stop.'

The project generated extraordinary enthusiasm. 'The expressions of kindness that we received were unbelieveable,' Hart reported, 'and the offers of money so generous that we sometimes actually became suspicious.' From the start, on 27 June, media coverage was excellent. Local radio stations gave the marchers generous amounts of air-time, and one, Radio Ceredegion, in Cardiganshire, followed Ednyfed Jones, a farmer from Tregaron, all the way to Hyde Park, giving daily updates on his and the party's progress. The propaganda value of these reports was slightly diminished by the fact that they were in Welsh, so that hardly anyone could understand them unless they were translated; nevertheless, it was good for everyone's morale to have so much attention.

The South Wales march, also, produced its characters, its heroes and heroines. David Barber, Huntsman of the Tivyside, had booked his first-ever holiday abroad, and was scheduled to leave for Majorca with his wife and daughter on Friday, 4 July. He nevertheless completed the six-day trek to Monmouth, arriving there on the evening of the third. Next morning he flew to Majorca; but so strong had been the bonds created on the march, so powerful the spirit, that he curtailed his holiday, bought an extra ticket, flew home to Luton on the eighth, landed at 5.30 pm, took a taxi, and caught up with the united marchers in time to walk with them on the ninth, the last morning.

Steve Collins, former huntsman of the Carmarthenshire Fox-hounds, had planned to walk, along with his wife Jan. Then he landed a job in Northern Ireland, which put him out of contention. Yet Jan was not deterred: paying her own way, she came over the water and walked every step of the route from St. Clears to London.

One of the most courageous was Joe Folder, aged fifty-eight: an oyster farmer ruined by an oil-spill, who now runs a nudist camp. For the first two days he walked in heavy boots, and 'totally destroyed' his size-thirteen feet. He then bought a pair of trainers – but they were scarcely large enough, and in any case the damage had been done. According to Adrian Simpson, his feet were 'an unbelieveable mess.' He had very deep blisters on his heels, and in trying to keep his weight off them by walking flat-footed, he strained his insteps, calves and thighs. For him the worst part of the journey was 'having to cheat in the escort vehicle – not being in control of one's life.' After the Monmouth leg he retired to his home in Pembrokeshire, but one day later he rang up the organisers to say that he was bringing his own van to use as an extra service wagon.

Another who could not stay away was Brian Warfield, driver of the back-up van, 'official plasterer of blisters and mother-figure.' Although severely disabled by damaged vertebrae, he did a brilliant job servicing the walkers' needs. He, too, went home when the column reached Monmouth, but next day he rang up Simpson and said, 'Oh, listen: I'm missing it so much. I want to go back and give Pip a hand' – which he did.

Dylan the Death – properly Dylan Evans, an undertaker from Ammanford, who in his spare time hunts a pack of mink hounds – intended to walk for two days, but ended up walking for six. Tasha Stevens, a groom from Haverfordwest, marched tirelessly the whole way to London, with her hair dyed a provocative shade of orange so that she resembled a fox. Michael Hughes, fifteen and still at school, was rather retiring when he started out with his elder brother Darren; but by the time he reached Hyde Park, frequent contact with the media had made this blacksmith's son blossom into something of a superstar: with his shades and laid-back air, he attracted reporters so effortlessly that people began referring to him and his brother as Liam and Nolan, after the Oasis Gallaghers. Earlier generations of the Hughes family had been miners, but there were no miners among the core walkers, for the simple reason that there is only one working pit left in the whole of Wales.

Beforehand, Simpson had expected that day-walkers (who often numbered up to 200) would 'burn our boys off.' On Day Two, the twenty-one mile stretch from Carmarthen to Trapp, near Llandeilo, the day-walkers did set 'one hell of a pace.' But the pride of the core marchers was such that they would not allow them to draw ahead, and, as Simpson put it, 'by Day Four we couldn't hold the core any longer. Their leader gave them a real speech about keeping together, and so on, but by the end of the day he'd thrown up his hands.' That morning – a Monday – the turn-out of day-followers had been small; but this delighted the core, who 'felt there was nothing to stop them,' and they covered the seventeen miles from Abercrave to Merthyr Tydfil by 2 pm.

For the first four nights it was possible for the core team to be driven home and sleep in their own houses or those of friends. Then, after Day Five, they passed the point of no return: too far from home to go back, instead they were sumptuously entertained by Sian Legge-Bourke at Penmyarth, her home on the Glanusk estate, near Abergavenny, standing on the side of a hill in a lovely park above the River Usk.

Many looked back on that night as the most memorable of their trip. Not only were all twenty-four of them entertained as guests in a large and comfortable country house: they knew that their hostess, besides being an exceptional fisherwoman, forester and farmer, was Lady-in-Waiting to the Princess Royal, and that her daughter Tiggy had looked after Prince Charles's children. Of greater immediate importance than these royal connections was the fact that they all sat down to a magnificent stew in the Rod Room, and ate and drank to repletion. Bill Legge-Bourke, Sian's husband, happened to be away, but she herself found the evening hilarious. Not knowing quite what the form would be, her visitors had all brought their sleeping bags with them; and when they found that there were beds for all, the only ones who used their bags were the men called upon to share doubles.

After finishing their route at Monmouth on the evening of Thursday, 3 July, the South Wales team was taken by bus to spend the night at various billets near Ashton-under-Hill, where the marchers from Machynlleth were arriving soaked and exhausted. The two parties did not see each other that night, but came together in the morning.

By then the march organisers, guided by Amanda Courtney, had realised that they must not merely hope for events which would appeal to the media. On the contrary, they must create them – and now they laid on a meeting in a spectacular setting. Fortunately the morning was fine; the place, a shelf of grass field on a hillside that commanded staggering views over the Vale of Evesham. Between 400 and 500 people gathered to witness the event, and there was a moment of intense emotion when the South Wales column came up over the hill behind a hedge and walked towards the Machynlleth party. As the two companies met, everyone shook hands and struck up with 'There'll be a welcome in the hillsides.'

That was the day on which, after long hesitation, the racing world threw its weight behind the marches, and behind hunting. Until then support from the equine fraternity had been distinctly luke-warm, but now the *Sporting Life* carried a full-page advertisement for the Hyde Park rally, sponsored by Tattersalls and the Jockey Club, and distinguished figures from the turf turned out in force. Among the company were the trainers David Nicholson and Barry Hills, jockeys past and present – Willie Carson, Adrian McGuire, John Oaksey, Peter Scudamore, Michael Hills, Chris Maude, Brendan Powell, Warren Marston, Richard Johnson, Nick Fitzgerald, who won the 1996 Grand National on Rough Quest – and representatives of the *Sporting Life* and *Racing Post*. When the united Welsh march set off, Nicholson walked for the whole of the day, as did Lord Oaksey. Finding himself beside Oaksey on a climb, Roger Hughes asked how he would describe the going – good to firm? – and got the terse answer, 'No. Hard!'

That night came another of the entertainments that the marchers would never forget: a magnificent barbecue given by John and Liz

Wills at their home, Kirkham Farm, near Lower Swell. Liz – Charles Mann's sister – had been working as a volunteer in the Marches Office, and so knew the core walkers' needs better than anyone. Now she not only laid on a splendid meal, but invited in a whole lot more guests who she thought would like to meet the heroes and heroines of the road. A hundred and eighty people crowded into a marquee on the lawn: the singing was so powerful that it drowned out the discotheque, and the imbibing so phenomenal that the nearby town of Stow-on-the-Wold was said to have been drunk dry of gin. Sue Morgan the post lady recorded that 'Pain, blisters, swollen ankles and tiredness were forgotten as we danced and drank and sang till late.' Someone else reckoned 'the more crippled they were, the harder they danced,' and the event became known, with good reason, as 'The Cripples' Ball.' Late that night Pip Jones got up out of bed to answer a call of nature and was so bemused – partly by carousing, partly by being in a strange room – that after blundering about for some time, unable to find the door, he walked into a wardrobe and laid open his right eyebrow.

By that stage of the trip the cameraderie in the column had become so tight and strong, and the jokes were so well established, that newcomers found it difficult to break into the group. Nevertheless, recruits were welcome – especially if, like Richard Hall, they made outstanding efforts to join in. A dairy farmer, Hall milked his cows every morning, drove out to join the march, and then at the end rushed home to milk again – an exacting schedule which he maintained for four or five days.

David Nicholson was so impressed by the spirit and dedication of the people he had walked with that on 5 July – a rest day, mercifully – he invited them all to Jackdaw's Castle, his newly-built training stables at Ford. There they were given a tour of the establishment and sat in the garden with cans of beer, glowing with yet another manifestation of the goodwill which so many country people felt towards their enterprise. Lunch was provided by the ladies of the Warwickshire Hunt, who laid on what Pip Jones described as 'a banquet – some feast' at the Heythrop kennels. Sitting on bales in an open shed, everyone tucked into salmon, beef, ham and colossal mounds of strawberries. The Heythrop's Huntsman, Anthony Adams, showed everyone round the premises. Then, after a peaceful, relaxed afternoon, he loaded the core marchers into a huge horsebox and drove them to Stow Rugby Club, where they watched the final test between the Lions and South Africa.

Day Ten, Sunday, 6 July, turned out one of the most memorable on any of the marches. In the background Amanda Courtney's skilled advocacy was having its effect: at both national and international level, the publicity bandwagon had begun to roll. In the press and on television, the new peasants' revolt was making headlines. Closer at hand, word had spread that the marches were generating an astonishing intensity of enthusiasm and comradeship. The result was that by 9 am on a glorious morning some 700 people had gathered in one of the Willses' fields to see the Welsh on their way, and in Stow, just up the hill, many more crowded into the market-place to watch the column arrive in town.

Just before they reached Stow, Sam Butler approached Heather Tylor saying he wanted to change the route through the Bicester country – her own – and divert through Oxford instead:

> He says it has to be my decision. I say I am too tired to decide, and he is welcome to change everything, as long as he does it all himself. He insists it is up to me. I am instantly reduced to tears and tell him I am too tired to make decisions. Poor Sam – all he needs. He goes over to David Jones and asks his advice. David says, 'Do whatever Heather wants.' Roy Savage moves menacingly up behind Sam and tells him to do whatever I want. David comes up to me and says they will all do what I want. I say I am too tired to mind *what* they do – and then we walk into Stow.

The Oxford option was dropped. But nothing could have beaten the reception the marchers got in Stow. The people in the square heard them first: faintly to begin with, then louder, the sound of Welsh voices singing ricocheted out of one of the narrow streets that lead to the square. In a few moments the whole place was a solid mass of people – 2,500 of them at least – with many bemused tourists trapped in the middle of the throng.

In the brilliant early sunlight David Jones climbed on to the bonnet of a Land Rover and made a short speech in which he said that he and his followers had been treated 'like kings and queens', and that he was marching for the benefit of generations to come. In another impassioned address from the same vantage-point, Sam Butler thanked the core marchers for their valiant efforts, and revealed that the value of the publicity which they had created was estimated at £2.5 million.

Inevitably, singing broke out. It started with Ian Hawkins, from Brecon. At home, he claims, he 'keeps threatening to join the Brecon Choir. They say they never turn anyone down – only try to make them better.' Now in Stow his *forte* was that he knew all the verses of 'D'ye Ken John Peel?', and in his wavering monotone he led the huge chorus steadily through it. 'So sad,' wrote Heather. 'More tears. Can't stop now. Would love him to sing at my funeral.'

As Geoff Bow launched into a Lakeland favourite, 'The Horn and the Hunter', the emotional voltage running through the crowd rose to new levels. 'To hear one voice leading John Peel and the fell song brought a shiver down the spine,' wrote Kirstie Wood. When the crowd took up 'Jerusalem', all over the packed square people made no attempt to hide their tears.

Now the crusade had really gathered strength. The Welsh contingent was more than sixty strong; at least 1,200 people joined the march as it left Stow, and several hundred stayed with it over the high Cotswolds, right to the day's finish.

Total strangers were constantly asking what they could contribute. In Stow a well-built, stocky man had come up to Pip and given him two boxes of bananas, one of apples, one of melons, one of oranges. At the lunch-time stop near Oddington he appeared again, this time with baskets of plums. 'He refused to take anything for them, and wouldn't even tell me who he was.'

Such generosity, coming from all quarters, continued to amaze the organisers. Another day a businessman turned up at lunch-time and somehow gained the impression that the core walkers were going to have to pay for their supper. That afternoon he rang the office and said, 'I honestly can't let these men and women find their own evening meal.' He was assured that they would not have to. 'Nevertheless,' he said, 'they've so inspired me that I'd like to pay for supper one night.' Whereupon he wrote out a cheque for £500.

Day Ten ended at Ditchley Gate, north of Woodstock. There, once again, the antis had mustered a small force: a dozen dark creatures clad from head to foot in black, including balaclava hoods, screaming obscenities, although with little conviction. They did not know that the man who wound down his car window to talk to them was Mark Miller Mundy, prime mover of the marches. But when he said quietly, 'Sorry, boys – you're last year's flavour,' their jaws dropped, and for a few moments they were dumbfounded, as the truth of what they had heard struck home.

David Jones took an equally dismissive view:

This policeman had been with us all day. Typical – a real, old-fashioned country copper. He walks up to the antis, and he says,
   'You're nothing but a bunch of dickheads.'
   'Why d'you say that?' asks one of them.
   'If you were anything of a man, you wouldn't be covering your face up like that.'
   Within minutes the copper's superior is on the radio, saying he's had a complaint.
   'Tell you what, Boss,' he says. 'The best thing is to come and see for yourself.'
   Ten minutes later, up arrives the riot van with an inspector and a load more coppers on board. One look, and *hwycck!* 'Off you go!'

By Day Eleven, for all their high spirits, many of the core marchers were in dire physical straits. Richard Williams was in such pain from his shins that he was lowering gin-and-tonic by the pint, seeking to numb himself from the waist down. As they battled on through Vale of Aylesbury country to Forest Hill, near Oxford, Sue Morgan the post lady was plagued by pulled tendons in both ankles, and Chris Maiden, Huntsman of the Berkeley, recorded that his legs 'really suffered.' Luckily the Marches Office, foreseeing that people would be in trouble, had arranged for physiotherapists to be present, and at the end of that day there were four specialists waiting to receive casualties. As Pip Jones reported, 'They had quite a few to practise on.'

On Day Twelve spirits were lifted by the appearance of Ann Mallalieu, the distinguished QC who had thrown her considerable intellect and influence behind the hunting cause. She walked throughout the long morning to lunch at The Shepherd's Crook, the pub at Crowell, near the foot of the Chilterns. The meal was paid for by the millionaire philanthropist, J. Paul Getty II, who, at Baroness Mallalieu's invitation, came down off the hills from his home near Stokenchurch to meet the marchers. They arrived an hour and a half late, and many of them were so tired that they lay down and went to sleep on the lawn of the old rectory, next door to the pub, which the owner had kindly said they might use. David Jones was busy strapping up Gail Greenhouse's sore shins when Getty appeared. Breaking off for a chat, he fell into a discussion about red kites, some of which had been released on Getty's estate a few years earlier. The two men talked about the threat to field sports in general, and Getty said firmly that he thought the government should leave them alone. Jones will never forget his parting remark: 'Why repair a glass that's not broken?'

Another stirring innovation, that day and the next, was that John Wingfield, a farmer who had marched from Machynlleth, was joined by his eighty-year-old father, who amazed everyone with his agility and stamina. As John remarked, 'before that, his most important march had been the retreat on Dunkirk.'

That night brought the footsore Welsh to the Chiltern village of Monkton Speen, and the end of their great solo effort. Many of the women had lasted better than the men. Anna Turner's hard training had certainly paid off. To Pip Jones's amazement, 'She'd come in for lunch, but she'd never think of resting. She just wanted to get up and sell the white T-shirts.' Heather Tylor had eventually put a precautionary bandage round one knee – which delighted the men, because at last they reckoned she was human – but even she was near the end of her tether. 'A very long day in the heat,' she wrote.

The last hour pretty desperate again. David Jones in agony, but keeps going. Gail, having walked brilliantly, is now suffering badly, and bravely finished the day on crutches. We are all very tired, but will get there now.

Relations between the northern and southern contingents had not been entirely harmonious: the northerners reckoned that the southerners kept walking too fast, and were suspicious whenever they saw some of them riding in their back-up van. The southerners felt that the northerners always went too slow. In the end, though, none of this mattered. Next the morning the whole party would join up with the northern and Cornish columns for the final advance on London. The finish of the marathon was in sight; and even the people on crutches were buoyed by the knowledge that their efforts had roused up a hurricane-force wind of support throughout the rural community.

Everywhere in Britain, country people's thoughts were turning to the rally. In Oxfordshire the farm manager of Preston Estates telephoned Jim Dance, Managing Director of Risborough Agriculture, main agents for John Deere tractors, and asked what he was doing on Thursday. Dance replied that he was going to Hyde Park, and taking three of his staff. 'Right,' said the farm manager. 'You've got our business for next year.'

CHAPTER SEVEN

Count-down to Hyde Park

For the marchers the main event of Wednesday, 9 July, was a major press conference and photo call at Hawthorn farm, high on the Chilterns near Great Missenden, laid on for 11 am by Amanda Courtney. All three columns were taken to the rendezvous by bus – but the northern group had been on the road hours earlier, as they needed to walk part of their day's route before breaking to face the media. They set out from Ramridge Farm at 6 am, and as they swung along through the Hertfordshire countryside, Mary Holt and her friend Sarah Morley amused themselves by playing 'Over the Cliff' – a simple girls' pastime in which, as they observed the three men walking in front of them, each in turn had to nominate which they would go to bed with, which they would marry, and which they would push over the cliff. Familiar though she was with the game, Mary felt there was something faintly grotesque about playing it at 6.45 am.

The press and photo-call was obviously a staged event, but none the worse for that. The three columns were decanted from their coaches at different points around the perimeter of a large, level field which had been partially cleared of hay, but was still dotted with big bales along one side. On their way to the rendezvous the Welsh bus had passed the Cornish, and Roger Hughes had found the abrupt glimpse of their western allies profoundly affecting: pins and needles ran up his arm, and he was suddenly close to tears, with 'a funny sense of achievement.' The northern group were the first to arrive, and were amused when they were told 'to hide'. As Sue Elms remarked, it is not that easy to conceal a fifty-four seater bus in a mown hay-field – but they kept out of the way for the time being.

Then, with a posse of reporters and television crews in position, out marched three little armies on converging lines of advance. A lone piper led the northern company; the Red Dragon banner fluttered at the head of the Welsh column, and Brian Webber carried St Pirian's flag, with its white cross on a black background, for the West Country contingent. True to form, the Welsh were singing as they came. For onlookers, it was easy to imagine that the flaming yellow T-shirts were suits of armour flashing in the sun, and that the scene was being set for the filming of some medieval epic: *Henry V*, perhaps; less easy to imagine the emotions of men and women meeting for the first time after prodigious individual efforts. Many recognised friends in other columns – Ed Tate set eyes on his brother Paul, who had walked from South Wales, for the first time in months – but strangers embraced freely, drawn together by feelings of communal triumph. 'Although we hardly knew one another,' Sue Elms reported, 'everyone was cheering and crying, shaking each others' hands.'

In the farmyard, before a handsome, timber-clad barn, the leaders made brief speeches. David Jones declared that he had never before had such a physically demanding assignment. He did not go so far as to admit that he had been using one crutch intermittently, but he did say, 'I never thought it would be so hard – and I walk for a living.' Then he added, 'If this Government can't stand up and listen to people like you, it'll be a very sad day.' Richard Williams, from under Snowdon, also pronounced himself knackered. 'My feet are killing me. My shins are killing me. I'm in a very bad way. But if I have to *crawl* into Hyde Park tomorrow, I tell you, I'll do it.'

David Latham, father-figure of the Cornish family, recalled the stormy night on Dartmoor, when thirty-five sodden marchers had crowded into the tiny farm kitchen. 'The lady said, "Come on in." There was hardly room to stand, but she gave us hot food. She gave us hot drinks. We left two inches of water on her kitchen floor. That's what this is all about.'

The indomitable Derek Cross was too modest to make a speech. Although pressed to do so, and hailed as 'an inspiration to us all,' he refused. By then he had increased his normal dose of painkillers from two a day to eight, and was taking anti-inflammatory tablets as well. Never in the course of 400 miles from Coldstream had he resorted to the sticks carried as emergency props in the back-up van: he had walked unaided every step of the way.

With speeches done, the media got a chance to interview core marchers. After weeks on the road, all the men and women looked magnificently fit, and the bilious yellow of their T-shirts sat more easily against deep tans than it had on the pale necks and arms of the start. Many of the men had put on weight. Some found to their consternation that they had gained half a stone or more; and although they hoped that part of it was extra leg muscle, they knew quite well that most was the legacy of phenomenal hospitality along the way.

Days of practice had turned many of the marchers into highly efficient communicators. Miller Mundy's original anxiety – that the crusade would be let down by inept utterances to the press – had never been realised. On the contrary, numerous core walkers had spoken out about their beliefs with ever-increasing fluency and conviction, and now they were able to reel off statistics with impressive despatch: that annual direct expenditure on country sports amounts to £3.8 billion, that country sports generate 60,000 full-time jobs, that they contribute £634 million to Government income in taxes and licences, that the rural community makes up only two per cent. of the voting electorate, yet manages eighty-five per cent. of the land . . . and so on. Several could quote freely from the Phelps report – the latest on fox-hunting – which suggested that hunting with hounds may well be the least, rather than most, cruel method of fox control. The Manns' office had provided yet more ammunition by working out that on sixty-five marching days, with an average of 200 people out every day, the total of miles walked to Hyde Park would be 260,000 – the equivalent of more than ten circumnavigations of the globe. Yet still the main argument of every man and woman was that they were walking for freedom of choice, for the right of a minority to be heard and respected.

All over the country, fresh volunteers had been coming forward with offers of help. A military-sounding gentleman called the office to say that although he was too lame to join one of the marches, he and his family were going to Hyde Park. But he wished, also, to render some practical assistance – and in the end, he did. On 9 July the Cornish column needed transport from Camberley to the press call at Great Missenden, leaving at 8 am. The office tried the army, to no avail. Nor were any coaches available at that time – the hour of the school run. Landed with the problem, the gentleman-volunteer found an out-of-commission bus, had it plated, licenced and insured, himself accompanied the West Countrymen to the press call – and paid for the whole enterprise himself.

The Cornish had already completed their march at Ascot, but for the other two columns there were still fifteen or so miles to walk. The Welsh, who were on route, merely had to turn right out of the farm gate and keep going; and although not morally obliged to do so, many of the West Country men and women went with them. The northerners, meanwhile, bussed back to the point where they had broken off, and set out southwards through Hertfordshire towards their finish under a flyover of the M 25 at Potter's Bar.

Everyone was tired, and nearly everyone was in some degree of pain. The day became exceedingly hot. But the walkers were spurred on by the knowledge that they were on the verge of completing huge personal triumphs – for many, the greatest of their lives – and ahead of them dangled the carrot of the rally next day. Some, like Roger Hughes, were afraid that Hyde Park might be a let-down, that not many people would bother to turn out: 'I had a nasty feeling it might be like a meeting in the village hall. You publicise it all over the place, and on the night you're the only one there.' Along with several others, he felt that any total below 100,000 would be a severe disappointment.

One or two were sceptical of the whole exercise. Steven Hill, who had walked from Machynlleth, felt that the marchers had been 'hiding behind a banner' all the way: 'We had such vague slogans on our shirts and signs that the unconverted would not have known what we were marching for.' It seemed to him that he and his fellow-walkers had been used merely 'as a build-up to the big day, to spread the word about Hyde Park.' As should be clear by now, this was an altogether too cynical interpretation of what had happened. Certainly the marches had acted as a build-up – and on a scale that nobody had dared hope for – but they had been planned all along as a huge statement on their own.

Everyone had plenty to think over. For those from farming backgrounds, it had been fascinating to journey through a variety of agricultural landscapes, moving slowly enough to observe them all at close quarters. Roger Hughes reflected on how he had set out through the high, lean sheep country of Central Wales, then dropped into the fat cornfields of Herefordshire, where the soil was brick-red and fertile beyond imagining. Going over Bredon Hill, he had been appalled by the number of stones lying on the ground – Cotswold limestone brash – and the same in the Chilterns, although there the stones were myriad pieces of flint and chalk. Yet he had admired the neat, brick-and-flint architecture of the Chiltern farmhouses and cottages. Especially in the later stages of their journeys, all three columns had witnessed at first hand the truth of the claim that field sports improve the environment: everywhere in the Home Counties people saw how landowners had planted woods, hedges and copses for shooting or foxhunting, and how these carefully-nurtured pieces of cover gave shape and variety to the landscape.

The target for the combined Welsh-Cornish march was Micklefield Hall, the home of Richard and Sarah Edmonds, whose 350-acre farm had been cut in two by the M25. The symbolic journey's end was Sarah's Bridge, a farm crossing over the motorway. As they reached the end of it, the marchers halted briefly, formed up in neat ranks and stormed across for the benefit of television cameras. Then they tied their banners to the fences, and were delighted by the volleys of horn-blowing and the flashing of lights that came up from lorry-drivers and motorists passing beneath them. Thereafter, it was only another quarter of a mile uphill to the hall.

The northern marchers, also, were aiming for the M25, but for an underpass rather than a bridge. They had walked much farther than anyone else, and they, too, were in a bad way physically. Spiderman Dave Brearley had torn the ligaments in one knee, lost two toenails, knocked one toe 'out of socket,' had more blisters than ever in his life, and walked the last 200 miles 'with both knees strapped up, both feet bandaged because they were so tender, and plasters on every toe.' He reckoned he had personally refuted the claim made by the League Against Cruel Sports that between eighty and ninety per cent of the population are against hunting: in all the 404 miles from Coldstream, he had counted a total of forty-two people who demonstrated some form of dislike or opposition.

101

As the column drew close to the motorway, Ed Tate and John Harrison were touched to the quick when their comrades asked them to 'potter up to the front.' For days – weeks – they had hung back, letting Paul Crofts set the pace; but now for the last mile they went forward into the lead – and so they came at last to their finishing point on the boundary of the London Borough of Enfield.

Under the flyover they stopped, in a moment of silence. Hearing mutters behind him, Harrison turned round and said, 'What are you buggers up to now?' Another moment's silence. Then, as Tate remembered it, 'a holler started from the back of the column and came rolling through. Pigeons, startled by the noise, poured out of the recesses of the motorway in dozens above our heads. John and I shook hands, and suddenly I realised that we'd done it. I walked across a few steps, and there I was in London.'

Coaches transported them a mile back to a field in the middle of Enfield Chase, where they waited for lifts to Micklefield Hall. For Harrison, that was the lowest point. He sank down against a car feeling 'absolutely shattered. I'd had enough. Not the physical side – I could have walked for ever. It was all the hype and the media, being nominated as spokesman day after day. You tend to take it to heart a bit. If my wife had appeared in the hay field at that moment and said, "Come on, let's go home," I'd quite happily have gone, and to hell with the rally.'

For days a horrible suggestion had been rife: that at journey's end everyone was going to have to drink champagne from one of Dave Clement's wellies. Sure enough, somebody produced a bottle and poured its contents into a boot – whereupon, in Tate's words, 'those who had the misfortune to be caught were invited to have a drink.' The experience, he reckoned, was 'the only feature of the march that left a bad taste in my mouth.' With an hour to spare, yet another benefactor offered the weary horde a swim in her pool, and in they all went. Sue Elms reckoned the scene one of the most memorable of her whole trip:

Luckily Di Barker and I were the first in – luckily, because those who didn't jump were thrown. There in the middle of the pool – at the shallow end, because he couldn't swim – was Derek Cross, taking a large swig of whisky from a bottle. As he pulled the bottle away, a huge grin spread over his face. He had done it. He had walked from Coldstream to London.

With all 136 core walkers gathered at Micklefield Hall, the scene was set for a phenomenal last-night revel. When Chipps Mann first approached the Edmondses, weeks earlier, she had asked if they could put up maybe half a dozen marchers. Sarah agreed at once – but gradually the numbers grew, to the point at which Richard postponed a fishing trip to the Outer Hebrides so that he could be present to help his wife entertain the horde. On the last day the count climbed higher and higher, so fast that Sarah had to keep flying in to the nearest Tesco to augment her supplies.

Richard was disturbed by the way in which many of the walkers were hobbling, and by the gory state of their feet. He saw that they had been through a major ordeal, and quickly came to admire their courage. He little realised that members of the northern column were plotting a mutiny: now that they had come so far, a faction was all for marching on, right the way to Hyde Park. Five or six walkers were against the idea, and they persuaded Charles Mann to come and talk the rest out of it. Mann insisted that any such plan would cause chaos and bring down the wrath of the police, possibly jeopardising the whole rally. In the end the ring-leaders backed down.

Tea on the lawn of the eighteenth-century house was itself a delight: 'Waited on hand and foot and don't have to move a muscle,' wrote Heather Tylor. 'Beautiful place, lovely evening.' Then people dispersed for showers and baths (some took to a large cattle trough), and on a perfect summer night, with no cloud in the sky, a tremendous party began.

A neighbouring farmer, Ron Higgs, had come in to run the bar. A friend, Mike Minoprio, an expert carver, sliced into a whole roast pig to launch the barbecue. Robin Hanbury-Tenison and Ann Mallalieu dropped in to make short, rousing speeches. There was dancing, singing, and inevitably – with Mary Holt present – fireball hockey. So riotous did proceedings become that in the morning many could remember little about what had happened. The endlessly good-natured hosts went to bed at about 1.30 am, leaving the lights on and the back door open; but a number of the revellers never got to bed at all. Eventually, around 4.30 am, the last of them fell asleep where they subsided – in the barn, in the old cricket pavilion, on straw bales or plastic fertiliser bags, under trees in the garden.

Richard Edmonds was astounded by their consumption of alcohol, particularly gin: a case of twelve bottles had been presented by Justerini & Brooks, and when it arrived he had eyed it hopefully, thinking that a few walkers wouldn't want much, and that perhaps eight or nine bottles might be left over . . . Alas, not a drop remained. Afterwards, he counted that night as 'one of the great, dramatic moments in the house's history' – and since the site had been inhabited for a thousand years, that was no ordinary tribute. For Heather Tylor, also, it was a night to remember:

> Eventually we all congregate round Pip's van with a bottle of whisky, and the boys tell jokes. They are very funny, and I am reminded yet again what a privilege it has been to share this unique holiday with a bunch of predominantly hunt servants from all over Britain. They are the nicest, funniest and politest people I shall ever meet.
>
> There is an underlying feeling of deep unhappiness among the terrier-men, who fear greatly their jobs will be sacrificial lambs in the game of hunt and politics. Now that it is all over, there is a kind of tension, hard to describe, tinged with sadness at the prospect of getting back to reality.
>
> The press are everywhere, sensibly taking their chance to interview the people who really matter in this debate – the people who know what they are fighting for, and whose livelihoods may well depend on the outcome of the rally tomorrow.

For Ed Tate, the most powerful impression left by the march was of 'the determination, the spirit, the essential goodness of the people who came down.' Far from being bloodthirsty savages, they proved themselves 'thoroughly nice' – a weak word, he agreed, but one which hinted at the true nature of a group 'who all wanted to contribute, to make things, to do things, to keep the countryside a diverse, alive and vibrant place.'

The sense of achievement among the rest of the core walkers is not easily described. Many felt, like June Moon, that they had made friends for life, and that some special bond had grown up between them. Richard Markham, a young hunt servant from the Belvoir Kennels, reckoned the experience had made him 'more open-minded about other people's ideas and livelihoods.' For Peter Earnshaw, a twenty-one-year-old groom from Devon, the whole march had been 'amazing. I realised how much people cared for and loved the great countryside they live in, and the terrible effect it would have on so many different people's lives, and on future generations, if they had none of this to look forward to.' Martyn Blackmore recalled the way in which 'everybody helped each other through hard and painful days,' and David Daly 'how men and women with a set goal had pulled together.' From the end he looked back to the beginning, and recalled how in Madron, at that first call of 'Let's go to London!' from Brian Webber, 'we all stepped out.'

As the walkers relaxed at Micklefield, a small, independent party of mountain bikers, also rally-bound, was rolling into London after a marathon ride from Northumberland. Not having the time to walk, four intrepid thrusters from the Haydon Hunt had decided to go on wheels, and set off southwards from Haydon Bridge, on South Tyne, on 5 July.

The idea came from Charles Nicholl, a fruit and vegetable producer – a former master who now follows the hunt on a mountain bike. With him went his wife Fiona, Iona Lawson, current Joint Master of the Haydon and a farmer on the highest point of Hadrian's Wall, and Hugh Baily, an accountant with business interests. Their sweeper, driving a Volkswagen van, was Nellie Faulks, wife of a judge and a former schoolmistress. She could not ride, because she was recovering from a broken leg, but acted as 'driver, navigator and road-side cafe operator, and also kept a brief record of the trip

Saturday 5 July The most mountainous and physically difficult stretch. To farm B & B at North Otterington in Yorkshire. Supper in pub revealed most regulars going to London. The biggest mixed grills in the world. Eighty-one painful miles.

Sunday 6 July Probably the worst day. Heavy traffic round York, and so flat in South Yorkshire there was no chance to freewheel and rest. B & B at Ragnall in Lincolnshire. A stray Newcastle United supporter in the pub cheered us a lot. Ninety-six very long miles.

Monday 7 July Longest day, but prettiest for villages, to the Ship at Oundle. Delight on discovering our neighbour Mrs Templer had sent £25 for us to spend at the bar. What a merry night! Also discovered huge blisters on the bikers' tender places. All Oundle going to Hyde Park. Ninety-eight miles.

Tuesday 8 July An easy day, but one of experimentation with various soothing nostrums from the chemist in Oundle. Stayed at House Beautiful B & B at Clophill, near Luton. Fascinating. Forty-nine miles.

Wednesday 9 July Left the bikers today: difficult to accompany them through London. Terrifying for me – traffic far worse than Hexham on a market day. Solved problems by chewing gum, leaning my elbow on the window and playing the radio very loud with a thumping beat. The traffic parted like the Red Sea! Hotel in Sussex Gardens, Paddington. Six flights up and no lift. The bikers arrive at 6.30, and my son Sam meets us in Hyde Park, where we drink a bottle of Famous Grouse lying on the grass. Sixty three miles.

No bad effort, to pedal 387 miles in five days – especially as the bikers were all on the wrong side of fifty.

Unknown to the marchers, the bikers and the many thousands who were preparing to head for London by car, bus and train, the BFSS rally team was in a state of crisis. On Monday they had received a letter from David Welch of the Royal Parks Agency which appeared to cancel many of the arrangements so painstakingly worked out over the past few weeks. The worst blow was his instruction that the start of the rally must be postponed from 11 am to midday, and that no music could be played through the amplification system. Another severe limitation was his decree that construction of the main stand might not begin until Thursday morning: by the park's rules, if building began on the previous evening, it would turn the rally into an event. Welch suggested helpfully that on the day, should people arrive in good time, they could always go shopping in Oxford Street. Meanwhile, he himself was off on holiday, and his deputies would take care of things in his absence. In cricketing terms, this was an unplayable delivery, which left the away team groping. Once again, everything was up in the air.

Once again Andrew Sallis, responsible for the sequence of events on stage, had to re-cast his entire programme. Energetic recruiting by the BFSS had lined up an impressive array of speakers, and already it looked certain that some of them would have to be dropped.

From the number of coaches booked in (913 by Monday) and private trains (twelve), the BFSS knew that at least 50,000 people had their sights set on Hyde Park. Rumour suggested the total was going to be nearer 100,000. The last thing the organisers wanted was that supporters should drift off along Oxford Street, as Welch suggested: they might get lost or distracted, and never return. It had become very important to the BFSS that the magic figure of 100,000 should be attained, and it seemed essential that, once people reached the park, they should stay there.

On Tuesday 8 July Michael Parker called a final conference in the offices at Kennington. Robin Hanbury-Tenison, Peter Voute, Simon Clarke, Andrew Sallis and Posy Coutts took part in what Parker called a 'What If?' meeting. 'What if a submarine surfaces in the Serpentine?' he suggested – and only just in jest, for he had sought to cater for every possible eventuality.

Across the Cavalry Parade Ground from the stand, facing it from a distance of four hundred yards, a Portakabin would be set up on scaffolding some thirty feet above the ground. This was the ELT, the Emergency Liaison Tower, positioned to give its occupants a view over the whole of the rally ground, and equipped with closed-circuit television so that they could watch areas out of their line of sight.

Attempts at disruption by antis had by no means been ruled out. In Parker's view, 'we had set up an organisation which we felt could deal with whatever might happen,' and the police had an evacuation plan, to be used in the event of a bomb threat or attack on the stage. Naturally they would not divulge any details, but common sense suggests that in an emergency they would have moved spectators deeper into the park, rather than blocking Park Lane and Marble Arch with overflow crowds. One excellent feature of the site was that it had no barriers round it, and so would be relatively simple to clear.

At the Tuesday meeting the programme of entertainment was drastically pruned. It was decided, with great reluctance, to drop the choruses from 'Jorrocks', since these, in the view of the Parks Agency, would be 'too organised.' This was a bitter blow for the producer, John Howard-Jones, and his cast from the Bicester with Whaddon Chase Hunt, who had been rehearsing twice weekly for the past couple of months. Out, also, went the jazz band and the singer Jackie Allen.

The weather had turned so hot that there was much discussion of water. How could enough drinking water be provided? It was almost too late to lay on adequate supplies, but Posy Coutts began to investigate the possibility of having human dispensers walking round, with jerricans on their backs. In any case, many casualties from heat exhaustion were expected.

It was impossible to tie up all loose ends – there were so many flapping around – but Parker did make one firm stipulation: it was no good the BFSS having several different people in charge of different parts of the rally, he said. On the day, one person must be in command, and that person must be in the control tower. If trouble broke out, instant decisions would be needed: if the BFSS representative in the tower had to radio for someone else to come up and analyse the situation, the moment might already be lost. The decision-maker could not be Robin Hanbury-Tenison, because he would be on the platform, directing events, introducing speakers and looking after VIPs; so, after discussion, it was decided that the commander on the day should be Posy Coutts, who had already spent much time liaising with the police and park officials: they knew her, respected her ability, and requested that she should be in charge.

After further negotiations with the Parks Agency, at the last minute the organisers obtained permission for construction of the stand and control tower to start on Wednesday evening – but only because they pushed hard for it, on the grounds of safety: if people had to work in the dark, before dawn on Thursday, they said, the chances of an accident would be much increased. The ban on amplified music remained in place, the Agency's point being that the rally would occupy less than a quarter of Hyde Park, and that it would not be fair to other users if excessive noise spilled out into the remaining three-quarters.

The organisers were disappointed, but hardly surprised, by the fact that the Prime Minister, Tony Blair, had felt unable to send the rally a message of good will. He had sent such a message to the Gay Pride rally, held in Hyde Park the previous Sunday; but now he took cover behind the Minister for Agriculture, Jack Cunningham, who responded to the BFSS's invitation with a vacuous generalisation: 'I am determined that the comments of people living and working in the countryside will be high on the Government's agenda.'

CHAPTER EIGHT

Six-figure Protest

Thursday, 10 July, dawned mercifully cool. After the blistering heat of the previous two days, rally-goers were relieved to find the sky overcast, with a fresh east wind blowing. During the morning the clouds gradually burnt off, so that by midday the sun was shining, but the temperature remained comfortable throughout the day: ideal weather for an outdoor gathering.

For some time rumours had been circulating that IFAW – the International Fund for Animal Welfare – was preparing a major advertising campaign, to be launched just before the rally in an attempt to undermine it and lessen its impact. In the run-up to the General Election IFAW had contributed £1 million to the Labour Party – a clear indication not only of the organisation's political slant, but also of its enormous wealth, most of which derives from America. Early in July, when a journalist got through to a junior executive of the fund, the woman confirmed that a propaganda campaign was in the offing – a fact promptly denied by one of her superiors. Now, sure enough, full-page or double-page advertisements appeared in all leading British newspapers. The expense was colossal: two full-page, black-and-white advertisements in the *Daily Telegraph* at £38,500 each, two in the *Independent* £15,500 apiece . . . even if IFAW obtained a ten per cent. discount by booking early, the fund spent more on trying to browbeat readers of the *Independent* alone than the entire cost of the marches.

It might as well have saved its money. All over Britain, at hundreds of farms and kennels and racing stables, arrangements had been made for skeleton staff to look after the animals while working people headed for London. Small offices and shops shut for the day. The entire town of Oundle, it was said, had closed down . . .

A commemorative map published by *Hunting* magazine gave an excellent idea of the mass descent on the capital. Like Chaucer's Canterbury pilgrims, people came in
from every shire's ende
Of Engelond
– as well as from Wales, Scotland, Ireland North and South, France and elsewhere. The final count of coaches clocked by Posy Coutts was 924. The Duke of Beaufort's Hunt alone sent twenty, the Warwickshire sixteen, the Bicester with Whaddon Chase fourteen, the Cattistock twelve, the VWH eleven, the Quorn and the Cheshire and the Pytchley ten apiece, the Fernie nine. Single buses came from the Rother Valley Working Terrier Club, from Tattersalls, from the Tregynon Fox Club, from the Talbot Inn at Knightwick, near Worcester, and from many private estates, not least Glanusk, where the South Wales marchers had been so finely entertained by the Legge-Bourke family. Of this contingent, nine had never been to London before, and when they emerged on to the streets of the capital, some of them were so nervous of getting lost that they held each others' hands. One old gaffer who *had* once made the trip was heard to remark of the double-decker buses, 'Last time I were yur, they buggers was running on gas.'

Besides the coaches, twelve special trains bore visitors painlessly to the metropolis – for several organisers had discovered how delightfully simple it is to hire rail transport. The Berkeley Hunt, for instance, wanted to take a thousand supporters to the rally, and after a few exploratory telephone calls Richard Merrett, the Hunt secretary, got through to Rail Charter Services in Derby, saying that on 10 July he needed to lift a thousand people from Gloucestershire to London. The best the charter company could offer was a train of thirteen carriages which would hold 640 people. This Merrett secured at a cost of £10,700 – not payable until the day of travel.

On the day an agreeably old-fashioned looking yet spotlessly clean set of carriages appeared at Cheltenham, complete with train manager, buffet, framed posters for seaside resorts on the walls, and a note saying that the rolling stock had recently been refurbished by apprentices. After pick-up stops at Gloucester, Stroud and Kemble, every seat was taken: seven hundred and three people squeezed themselves on board, and during the run to Paddington the atmosphere became highly festive. One reason was that the travellers had brought along liberal supplies of alcohol; another that the fare was only £10 return – about a quarter of the regular full rate, and little more than a third of the cheapest normal day return. Yet the main cause of high spirits was simply that people felt they were off on a great adventure, taking part in a great crusade. Five buses, meanwhile, collected more Berkeley passengers from different pickup points and took them to Earl's Court, where white-tabarded BFSS stewards met them and directed them on to the right tube line. The 203 bus passengers each paid £7 return, and the net deficit on transport was met from hunt funds.

Thousands more people came in on scheduled trains, and main-line stations naturally became busier than usual; but the atmosphere everywhere remained remarkably cheerful. At Euston the wife of a senior diplomat found herself surrounded by stewards and policemen. She asked one officer what was going on, and was told about the rally. 'Normally, when we do these rallies, we get sworn at and told to mind our unspeakable business,' the bobby said 'But this is a very different crowd. They're all wishing us happy good morning, and saying what a grand day it is to be going to the park.' At which the old lady changed her plans, went to Hyde Park, and afterwards declared that it had been the second most memorable day in her life.

Some people had made phenomenal efforts to attend – and few journeys were longer than that faced by a party of deer-stalkers, gamekeepers and ghillies who came down from Sutherland and Caithness. By the time they boarded a coach booked by the BFSS at Inverness at 8 pm on Wednesday, several of them had already been on the road for a couple of hours. They then drove through the night, picking up more passengers on the way down, and reached Hyde Park at 7.30 am on Thursday. Their driver managed to find a place inside the park, within a few hundred yards of the rally site, but a man from the Agency promptly came on board and charged him £100 for the privilege. A whip-round among the party produced the necessary cash, and the men from the far north were free to wander through the empty park, not knowing was was going to happen, but unable to imagine that the place was about to be invaded by the biggest crowd any of them had ever seen.

Out at Micklefield Hall, after the excesses of the night, the core marchers were struggling to pull themselves together. Many got no more than two hours' sleep before they came groggily round to find television crews already setting up equipment for live broadcasts. Sarah Edmonds had been up since 4.30 cooking a tremendous breakfast, and by the time the walkers boarded coaches at 8.30 am, they were on their way to recovery (an energetic clean-up had left the scene of their revels spotless). But then, to their consternation, they found themselves decanted into No 2 Park Street, an empty office building about ten minutes' walk east of the rally site, and confined to barracks there for the duration. It was sensible enough that they should stay out of sight, and not be seen prematurely by the crowd, or attract unwelcome attention from antis. All the same, it was irksome to be stuck inside, in rooms bare of furniture, not knowing exactly what was going on outside.

'All the boys, very tired, lie curled up on the floor against one another, rather like hounds on the benches after a long day's hunting,' wrote Heather Tylor. 'Someone passes round a huge tray of smoked salmon, which is instantly rejected by all bar myself. They certainly don't appreciate that sort of rubbish.' Their best contact with the outer world was a messenger who took orders for newspapers, milk, fruit, cigarettes and so on, and ran errands up to a shop on the corner. Rumour has it that one of the prisoners asked, and was refused, permission to visit his tailor – but most of the requests were more mundane.

As the time to leave drew near, Sue Elms found the atmosphere becoming 'really electric. The Welsh lads and lasses had gone down into the foyer and were singing "We'll keep a welcome in the hillsides," and although we were two floors above them, the walls and floor were vibrating with the noise. It was very emotional, and tears were already starting to flow.'

In the park, meanwhile, there had been frantic activity round the main stand, as workmen scurried to complete the installations. They had started at 4 am, and at 7.30 it looked as though they had no chance of completing the stage in time. The Parks Agency had stipulated that all vehicles must be clear of the site by 8 am, and right up till then fork-lift trucks were whizzing in all directions, until Agency staff ordered them off by radio.

As the first visitors wandered in, they saw no signs of haste: it was evident that preparations had been made for a major invasion – portable lavatories lined up in serried ranks, caterer's vans sorting themselves out – but the prevalent impression was one of serenity, with the white county balloons floating above grass made exceptionally green by recent heavy rain.

Along with most of the organisers, Posy Coutts had arrived on site at 6 am, to sort out marshals and stewards at briefings, and settle dozens of details in the VIP enclosure. She was so busy all day that after a bacon buttie at 6.30 she had nothing more to eat until she found 'a piece of fruit in my Pimms at six in the evening.' Apart from herself, the team in the control tower consisted of a senior police officer, the heads of the fire and ambulance services, Vivienne Roberts, representing the Parks Agency, Kevin Eld from Unusual Services, Brian Blake, the Safety Officer from the Westminster City Council, and Michael Parker.

Through mobile phones and radio the BFSS representatives were in contact with police on the ground and with the stage; the police in the tower could also monitor traffic on all the roads round the park, as well as in Underground stations and underpasses – potentially dangerous bottlenecks, if any sudden movement developed in the large crowd. Throughout the rally police manned desks inside the control tower, but Coutts, Eld and Parker spent much of the time standing outside on the scaffolding, watching through binoculars.

Kevin Eld and Brian Blake were enormously experienced at handling this kind of event, and Coutts was familiar with the military system of signals in use to designate the state of alert: green for normal, up to amber (without the crowd being aware of it) if trouble threatened, then up to red if a decision to evacuate were taken. On the ground, the security staff from Showsec were all professionals, fully briefed on evacuation pocedures, and the BFSS had a far-reaching security operation of its own: stewards on the coaches would report to a supervisor if they saw anything they did not like, and similarly among the crowds they would report to the twenty supervisors who had radios. The hope was that BFSS people, being more practised than Showsec staff at spotting antis, would identify trouble-makers more quickly. (BFSS Head Office had asked local organisers to appoint a steward for every coach, and had sent out yellow tabards in advance. One organiser, receiving a jiffy-bag through the post, called in the bomb squad, only to find that the packet contained nothing more sinister than a tabard.)

Thus the background organisation was highly effective. The trouble was that, even now, no agreement had been reached about the programme, and Parker spent much of the morning in urgent discussion with Vivienne Roberts about what could or could not be done on the platform. She, coming into the picture at a late stage, was in an awkward position: she knew that this was not a normal, run-of-the-mill rally, and yet she had not taken part in all the earlier meetings. Again and again she said she did not want a particular item on the programme because it would set a precedent.

At 10.30 Parker called Posy across and said, 'Look – I'm going to keep talking to her, but you've got to decide whether you're going to follow the rules or not. It's your final call.' Over the radio Posy got Andrew Sallis and Charmaine Goodchild (Pacesetter's Production Manager) together and asked them to draw up a contingency plan. 'If we can't start till twelve, you have to start working on your feet now,' she told them. 'See what speeches you can take out, and how you can shorten the programme.'

The time was past 10.30. Sallis already had people lined up behind the stage, ready to go on in fifteen minutes. In spite of acute pressure, he remained calm and began to shuffle his options. Behind the stage, Parker called Posy over again and said, 'I think I've got her to accept the fact that we're starting at eleven, but only with warm-ups.' At 10.50 Posy called Sallis and told him. 'My decision is that we *can* have people on stage at eleven, but they *must* start speeches by saying that the real programme doesn't begin till twelve, and they *must* finish by saying, "Thankyou very much for listening to a warm-up." '

Naturally she wanted to inform Robin Hanbury-Tenison what she had decided, and ask urgently what he thought she should do about music; but he had temporarily had gone off the air, and again she had to take a decision herself. It was 'No music till later.' Her reasoning was that 'if they did pull the plugs on us and knocked the microphones out before the speeches proper had even started, everything might be lost.' There was also the question of money. The BFSS was supposed to have put down a £25,000 bond, and only through an administrative error on the part of the Parks Agency had they failed to do so. Now the organisers were afraid if they broke too many rules, they might forfeit all or part of it. Still nobody knew for certain how they stood. In Simon Clarke's recollection, 'Behind the stage, there was complete chaos. Nothing was black and white: all grey. It was order, counter-order: the fog of war.'

Just before 11 am Hanbury-Tenison arrived from an appointment, extremely keen that horns should play *and* be amplified. Posy discussed the idea with Charmaine, and decided that one English hunting horn could go out over the loudspeakers, but that if massed French horns were blown, they would constitute music, because they were a group, and playing tunes.

So, move by move, the cat-and-mouse game continued and the stage stuttered into life. In a brief introductory address Hanbury-Tension welcomed all-comers, particularly the marchers. 'I don't need to tell that they have caught the imagination of Britain,' he said. 'These brave marchers have awakened the countryside.' The message to Parliament, he went on, was 'Listen to us.' 'Would you like to say with me, "Listen to us"?' – and back came a thunderous roar: 'LISTEN TO US!'

Next on to the stage – demoted to a warm-up role – was Neil Greatrex, President of the Union of Democratic Mineworkers. To have secured the miners' leader was in itself a coup, and he played some strong cards by suggesting that a ban on field sports would wreak greater social havoc than the collapse of the mining industry had already created. After him came Glyn Pearman, farmer and game farmer, who described how he had planted trees and hedges on his land 'because field sports and country life are so important to me.' Then came Robin Page, conservationist and writer, Lord

Wakeham, Chairman of the British Horseracing Board, and Sir Thomas Pilkington, Senior Steward of the Jockey Club, all following each other in quick-fire order. The good humour of the crowd owed much to the Master of Ceremonies, Maurice Askew, a stout, Jorrocks-like, red-faced printer from Doncaster, whose reassuring Yorkshire accent and jolly manner effectively concealed the confusion prevailing behind the scenes.

Still people were flooding into the park. They were walking in long crocodiles from Paddington Station, and pouring up out of tube-exits. The BFSS's arrangements proved admirable: the rally-goers were delighted to be met off coach or train and be shepherded with such attention to detail. With the staff of London Underground going out of their way to help, the inward flow built up smoothly into a torrent – and so good was the organisation that normal London traffic, whether vehicular or pedestrian, was scarcely impeded.

Almost all the crowd came in country clothes: few of the men wore jackets, and fewer still ties. Bright shirts and dresses gave the crowd a festive air – and several thousand people were wearing the white T-shirts with green lettering on sale from the BFSS. (The park regulations prevented the distribution of these on site, but more than a thousand were sold, at £6 apiece, in the bus park at Wembley alone.) Even so, there were some who had fixed ideas about correct attire: one was an old boy from the Berkeley Vale who normally never ventured farther than his local, to which he rode on an ancient bike for a pint of cider, wearing scarecrow clothes. At the prospect of going to London, however, he decked himself out in shirt, collar, tie and jacket.

On the special trains, on the coaches and at points immediately outside Hyde Park, BFSS stewards and helpers had been handing out little, round badges bearing the words 'I WAS THERE' in green on a white background. When all 100,000 badges had gone, an announcement was made: there were already 100,000 people on the rally ground. A great cheer went up: the target had been reached, and passed – for streams of late-comers were still arriving, many of them city workers in business suits. (It was said that several merchant banks had positively ordered executives to attend.) The final estimation was 120,000. One of the oldest present must have been Monsignor Gilbey, who had come from the Travellers' Club on the eve of his ninety-sixth birthday. Only a decade behind him was the veteran stalker and hunting woman, Lorna Schuster, accompanied by Tim Healy, head stalker from Glenkinglas, her deer-forest in Argyllshire. In the family there were jokes about how Healy would have to keep her on baby reins, so that she did not get lost in the crowd, but in the event she managed perfectly – and Healy reckoned his own long journey from the Highlands a hundred times worth-while: 'It was astounding. The people all looked like human beings.'

Together with a couple of colleagues, Roger Hughes had been released from 2 Park Street at about 10.30 am to go and get press passes, so that the core marchers would be able to stay in the VIP enclosure behind the main stand after they had made their appearance on stage. When he returned to the office building, the pent-up core anxiously asked how many people there were in the park.
'A hell of a lot,' he told them.
    'Well – how many?'
    'A *heck* of a lot.'
They suspected he was exaggerating, but he promised he was not: they were in for a big surprise. Their own numbers suddenly increased by eleven when Chipps Mann decided to create the volunteers who had staffed the office honorary core walkers, and issued them with yellow T-shirts so that they too could receive the plaudits of the crowd.
    David Jones had been chosen to lead the delegation which would carry a letter to the Prime Minister in Downing Street, and he had gone off for security vetting before the party left. In his absence Roy Savage took charge of the Welsh walkers, and as they were preparing to leave for the park, he called for silence and made a little speech, presenting Pip Jones with a brass figure of a horse and plough on a wooden plinth, personally inscribed to thank him for his outstanding efforts on the column's behalf. Unknown to Pip, the marchers had had a whip round, and on a rest day two of the girls had found the present in Bourton-on-the-Water. As he received the memento, for the first time since leaving Machynlleth he was speechless and bereft of a gag.

Joanna Clapton (right) with support bus.

Cornish march. Jo Latham's surgery.

Robin Hanbury-Tenison.

Baroness Mallalieu.

Mark Miller Mundy and Chipps Mann.

Top: Dave
Clement and
Wellies.
Middle: Ashton-
under-Hill. The
Welsh marchers
unite.
Bottom: Brian
Webber leads the
Cornish marchers
from the Two
Bridges Hotel on
Dartmoor.

Lord Steel with Sarah Morley and George Bowyer.

Champagne goes into Dave Clement's boot.

Hyde Park. Amie Pascoe and Brian Webber.

The Northern march reaches the M25.

'Only a few could have put this together.' Three of the organisers: Charles Mann, Mary Eames and Posy Coutts (far right).

Welsh columns merge at Ashton-under-Hill.

Cornish marchers at Longparish House, Test Valley, Hampshire.

George Bowyer sings his Countryside Song. Sarah Morley in cap.

Core marchers arrive at the rally, 10th July 1997.

At last it was time to go. As the core marchers walked the half-mile to the edge of Hyde Park, well-wishers called out greetings – although some refused to believe they had come on foot all the way from Scotland. Then, after a wait just inside the park railings, they started down the long corridor of security barriers that led to the VIP enclosure behind the stand. Suddenly there were people, five and ten deep, yelling out at them in excitement, trying to grab and kiss them. Sue Elms reported:

When at last the piper set off on his bagpipes, that was it. Going down that avenue – I have never known a feeling like it. Total adrenaline! I felt like I had climbed Everest, I was so proud that we, the marchers, had done what we set out to do – to show the people of this country that we care passionately for our way of life.

People were cheering us, crying, clapping, screaming, waving their arms. It was unbelievable, hard to keep walking. You just wanted to stay for ever and say thankyou to everyone. Then I saw some of our hunt followers. They were shouting our names. I ran over and they grabbed me, crying 'Well done!' Grown men had tears in their eyes. Lasses had tears streaming down their faces. We walked on. Suddenly more people I knew: more hugs tears and kisses. The stage was growing nearer. But still the noise carried on.

The approach was stirring enough. Yet it was nothing to what followed. For every core walker, going up on the stage was the experience of a lifetime. None of them had ever seen 120,000 human beings in one mass. Still less had any of them been hit by the admiration, the gratitude – the *love* – of that many people, coming at them in a colossal wave.

Brian Webber – a member of the Downing Street delegation – was by then wearing the brand-new, lightweight, summer black-smith's apron generously presented by the Suffolk firm Gibbins. He had been waiting with his colleagues, confined for security reasons to the VIP enclosure:

Amie Pascoe, myself and one other girl went on to the stage to greet the rest of our core. Standing on the ground, it was like

119

being on a racecourse, watching a goodish crowd against the rails on the far side. Then suddenly we were eleven feet in the air and looking out over twenty-five acres of solid faces. It stopped me stone dead, and the next thing I knew, tears were rolling down my cheeks.

Another marcher thought that the crowd looked like an ocean of faces, 'going on over the horizon,' and Heather Tylor found it terrifying – 'Never seen so many people in my life. Can't wait to run off.' But if the sight of 120,000 people had a physical impact, so, even more, did the noise when the multitude gave tongue. No sooner had Webber gained the stage than a great bellow went up, and he knew the other core marchers were on their way:

The Northern lads came up first, then the Welsh, then our Cornish contingent, with Neil Mathieson carrying the flag. He said in a loud voice, 'Here y'are, Boss. You take it out front.' When I walked to the front and held the Cornish flag high, the ROAR that came back was a truly physical thing. And at the back I could hear them shouting, 'Uggy! Uggy! Uggy!', the old Cornish rallying call.

One man who did not flinch was George Bowyer, who, though not on the official programme, had been told that he must sing his Countryside Song. At the last minute he nearly fell foul of the internecine warfare raging on and behind the stage: while Maurice Askew was urging him to start, a girl with head-phones and a clipboard was hissing, 'Get off! Get off!' and the disc-jockey Simon Bates, one of the masters of ceremonies, was trying to hustle all the marchers away. But start he did, unaccompanied: for once the microphones were on, and even though they did not pick up the voices of the northern marchers, who came in with him for the choruses, the song really got the crowd going.

Out in Kennington, Peter Voute was maintaining a lonely vigil in the BFSS offices. At the weekend well-wishers had broken three windows by throwing stones, and now the building was ringed by police, with a small force of fourteen antis corralled on the pavement across the road. Inside, Voute had been on station since 6 am, helped by a small bevy of girls. At about 10.30 he began to get telephone calls from people held up by heavy traffic on the M4 and M40, and worried they would not reach the park in time. All he could do was to reassure them – and in the end, nobody arrived too late.

On the site, the huge crowd were blissfully unaware of the highly-charged exchanges zipping back and forth over their heads between control tower and stage. They realised that somehow things were not quite right, and they were puzzled by the continual references to 'warm-ups' in the opening speeches. But they ascribed the evident deficiencies of the sound-system to the incompetence of the technicians in charge, or the inadequacy of the equipment, and they remained incredibly well-behaved – in Michael Parker's view, 'uniquely so.' In all his long experience, he said, he had never seen a gathering of that size so good-natured. Everyone noticed the friendly atmosphere: the police appreciated it particularly. As one mother said, you could have walked through the throng with a baby in your arms and felt perfectly safe. If nothing else, the event demonstrated conclusively that field sports enthusiasts are not bloodthirsty monsters, but patient, civilised, ordinary people. They never pressed to the front with the hysterical abandon of audiences at pop concerts, desperate to be close to the stage: perhaps because country folk are used to open spaces, and like to have room around them, they kept their distance from each other, tending to stand in rows, with a gap between one line and the next. Even at the height of the rally it was still possible to walk through the crowd.

Nevertheless, people could not help being irritated by the fact that they could not hear the speeches. Some speakers were being amplified, but the sound-system was turned down so low that voices did not carry far. From the back people began to yell, 'WE CAN'T HEAR!' Further annoyance came from a police helicopter which kept circling overhead, drowning out the speakers' voices.

The thirty-three members of the Downing Street delegation had been carefully chosen to represent the widest possible range of rural occupations: among them were six core marchers, and David Jones had been selected as the man to present the letter, which read as follows:

The Rt Hon Tony Blair, MP,
No 10 Downing Street,
London SW1A 2AA.

Dear Prime Minister,

Many tens of thousands of people who live in, work in and enjoy the countryside have come to London today. We have come to the Capital because we are increasingly concerned that rural opinion is not being heard and that real damage may be done to the countryside if those who look after it are not listened to now.

Such is the strength of feeling that many of us have walked from Scotland, the North, Wales and Cornwall. The response from the public during our journey has been overwhelming in its support for our cause. For most of us who have marched here our jobs, our homes and our families' livelihoods in the rural areas are at stake. Prime Minister, we look to you, and the Governmment, to safeguard them.

Many people have had to stay at home to look after animals but would also have wanted to have their say. As the numbers in Hyde Park show today, the countryside is more united than ever and those who endeavour to divide us will not succeed. Please listen to what we have to say.

Country people are part of the One Nation you wish to create. We, who care for the countryside, will support you in your goal. Our way of life is distinct and is integral to the well-being of the rural areas of Britain. We in turn look to Her Majesty's Government and Parliament to safeguard our rural future.

May we count on you to ensure that our nation is not divided?

Yours sincerely,

Bob Baskerville, *Veterinary Surgeon,* David Jones, *Professional Huntsman,* Jemima Parry-Jones, *Falconer,* Ian Sumerell, *Gunsmith,* Brian Webber, *Blacksmith,* Martin Bertram, *Shepherd,*

Peter Hutchinson, *Tailor*, Sally Armstrong, *Caterer*, John McCririck, *Racing Correspondent*, Diana Brodie, *Greyhound Trainer*, Ednyfed Jones, *Welsh Hill Farmer*, Amie Pascoe, *Student*, Scott Thompson, *Ferreter*, Giles Wheeler, *Professional Huntsman*, Nicola Germany, *Forester*, Ian Mackie, *Feed Merchant*, Francisco Cardona, *Publican/Caterer*, Dennis Davis, *Bootmaker*, Roger Milsom, *Farmworker*, John Robilliard, *Pigeon Racer*, Robert Thornton, *National Hunt Jockey*, Willie Carson, *Flat Race Jockey*, David Byas, *Former Yorkshire Cricketer*, Thomas Scott, *Point-to-Point Jockey*, Sion Aron, *Farmers' Union – Wales*, John Harrison, *Professional Huntsman*, Chris North, *Gamekeeper*, Beth Scott, *Groom*, John Turner, *Fisherman*, Sidney Free, *Saddler*, Robin Dale, *Hedgelayer*, Howard Richardson, *Horse-box Manufacturer*, John Fretwell, *Union of Country Sports Workers*.

The evening before, John Harrison had been on his knees. Now, at the rally, he was 'flying', and when Patrick Martin, co-huntsman of the Bicester, blew the delegates away from the stand on his horn, the crowd's roar 'was like we'd scored a goal at Wembley.' The open-topped bus had been found in Bournemouth by members of the Portman Hunt, driven up to London during the night, and parked in the North Carriage Drive of Hyde Park under security guard. In the morning it was lavishly decorated, to a scheme devised by Ian Farquhar, Joint Master and Huntsman of the Duke of Beaufort's, its many embellishments including the Piccadilly Hunt banner from 1949. Besides the human delegation, it carried hunting dogs of every description – foxhound, beagle, greyhound, lurcher, terrier – as well as ferrets and a hawk, and the hounds sat up on the seats like people. The bus was thus an echo of the BFSS's original plan to send a full-scale agricultural procession to Downing Street.

When Harrison boarded the vehicle, he went right to the front of the top deck and stood there beside the Union Jack, all the way. 'We'd come that far. We'd done that much. There were over 100,000 people in the park. To drive through London knowing that was quite fantastic. I thought, "I'm buggered if I sit down and hide. I don't care who sees me now." I thought, "All right, antis.

You have a good look and see what you're trying to stop. See how you're faring."'

The antis were there, all right. At the Whitehall end of Downing Street the delegation ran into a white-hot blast of hatred. The police had corralled sixty or seventy of the opposition behind crush barriers: as usual, they were screaming 'Murdering swine! Bloothirsty bastards!' and barely printable obscenities. They were also whistling and seeking to intimidate members of the delegation by taking still photographs and video footage. Harrison waved at them and laughed. To him it was 'like day and night, as if we'd come from a massive party straight into a war zone.'

Only six of the delegates were allowed off the bus, to walk along Downing Street and hand in their letter. As David Jones went down the stairs, an inspector said, 'No one's getting off the bus.'

'*I'm* getting off the bus,' Jones told him.

'They're pretty noisy.'

'I don't give a shit. I'm not frightened of *them*.'

Jones saw that Beth Scott, the young girl groom, was looking scared. He said to her, 'You just get off and stay with me. Don't worry about anything.' Then he found Brian Webber beside him: 'That blacksmith from Cornwall got off and said, "I reckon you and me can handle this lot, Dave."' With that, the party of six set out through the iron gates and along Downing Street. The bus, meanwhile, made a circuit of Trafalgar Square, and Harrison thought how beautiful London looked in the bright sunshine.

With the letter handed in through the door of No 10, Jones and his party came back past the anti-terrorist barrier that lifts up out of the road, back to the gates. The inspector asked them to stay inside until the bus had turned round. Webber said, 'Well, dammit, there aren't that many of them. Let's go out and talk to them.' But the inspector said, 'No sir, I'm sorry. We don't know what there might be in the crowd.'

So, with a ring of eight police officers round them, the party marched out into the centre of Whitehall, where five police cars were parked head-to-tail, in two lines about five feet apart, forming a short corridor. As they walked down it, a woman ran along outside the cars, screeching insults. 'Look straight forward,' Jones told Beth. 'Take no notice of her.'

The bus ferried them back to the top of Park Lane, and again they walked down the corridor to the stand, to another ovation when they re-appeared on stage. By then the VIP enclosure had filled with celebrities of every size and shape. Invitations had been sent to all Members of Parliament: no Labour member had accepted – though some may have been present in the crowd outside – but prominent Conservatives were everywhere: William Hague, Michael Heseltine, Nicholas Soames, Lord Tebbit. The Liberal Democrats were represented by Lord Steel and Alan Beith, the Scottish Nationalists by John Swiney, Plaid Cymru by Cynog Dafis (who spoke from the platform) and the Ulster Unionists by Willie Ross. Politicians apart, there were Jeremy Irons, Terry Biddlecombe, Willie Carson, David Bellamy, Auberon Waugh, Tiggy Legge-Bourke, Clement Freud, Freddie Forsyth. The actress Paula Hamilton caused a stir when she stood too close to a ferret and was bitten in the neck, but she laughed the injury off with admirable aplomb. The most striking figure on view was that of Nell Stroud, the ring-mistress, who paraded in top hat, scarlet tail coat, fish-net tights and full circus make-up.

In speaking from the stage, no one raised a louder roar than David Jones, who, having paid tribute to the core walkers, announced, 'This is the last peaceful march, and this is the last peaceful rally.' Sam Butler also praised the marchers with an eloquent tribute and prophecy:

> The atmosphere and the feeling as we came down from Scotland, in from Wales and up from Cornwall have been awesome. These men and women have created a bond. It will take something out of this world to ever, ever split them up. I suspect, now, it will take something awesome to ever split you country people of all walks of life.

Butler called on the crowd to salute Mark Miller Mundy, who conceived the idea of the marches – but he, almost overcome, could only say, 'It's an amazing sight! Amazing stuff! Thankyou!' Lembit Opik, Liberal Democrat Member of Parliament for Montgomeryshire, delighted the audience with a flurry of short, sharp punches:

Foxes may look cuddly and sweet, but so does Mike Foster. Let's face it, they're both a bit of a pest. Mr Foster, look around. This is a message to you from the British countryside. Tony Blair, look around. Ask yourself, 'Are you so sure you are right?' Why have over 100,000 people come to London today if you are so very right?

We haven't come here to dictate the urban way of life. We've just come to be heard. Is that too much to ask?

Cynog Dafis, the Plaid Cymru MP, echoed many others when he said, 'It's an issue of individual freedom. There has to be a very, very good reason indeed to legislate, to make an activity pursued by so many people into a criminal activity.' Next into the breech was Maitre Pierre Daillant, diminutive President of the European hunting organisation, FACE. His speech was short, but much to the point – 'I give you greetings and support from the countrymen of the rest of Europe. Long life to countryside, long life to country sports'. When he ended, 'And in my own language, *Vive la campagne! Vive la chasse!*', he drew two thunderous echoes: *'VIVE LA CAMPAGNE!* roared 120,000 voices. *'VIVE LA CHASSE!'*

In a terse, hard-hitting broadside the naturalist David Bellamy declared himself an East-Ender – 'not one of those plastic ones you see on the bloody telly these days, but a real one' – and lamented the decline of Britain's forests, wild flowers and wild-life. Many of the crowd, apprehensive about what views he might hold on field sports, were amazed to hear him come out strongly in favour of hunting, because of the diversity of wildlife and landscape that it preserves:

Now I think you're bloody cruel, and I couldn't do it myself; but I'm very glad you're there doing it! Because the real cruelties are the battery hens and the veal crates and the whole of factory farming . . .

Now please, please Mr Blair, as you think, think about the fact, the fact of labourers in the field, and keep this country bio-diverse and sustainable. Welcome your marchers. The long march has just begun.

Yet the speech of the day came from Ann Mallalieu, a striking figure with her fair hair and red jacket. Whatever else the crowd might have missed, they heard her every word. Her eloquence and passion were spell-binding: as someone said, 'If you'd dropped a pin while she was speaking, you'd have heard it hit the grass.' From her opening line, her words had a far-reaching, heroic ring:

Farmers have left their haymaking, farriers have left their forges, racehorse trainers have left their runners at Newmarket. Doctors, nurses and vets have changed their shifts to be here. Judges have adjourned their cases for the day. Children have taken a day off school, and countless country firms and businesses have closed or are running on skeleton staff. People who are old and people who are ill have travelled many miles, some setting out before dawn. Others, as we've just seen, have been travelling for days through heat and rain, through pain and discomfort, from all parts of the United Kingdom and beyond. Great sacrifices have been made by many of the people who were determined to be here. . .

We have come here for one reason. We cannot and will not stand by in silence and watch our countryside, our communities and our way of life destroyed for ever by misguided urban political correctness.

This rally is not just about hunting. Many, perhaps most, of those here today don't hunt themselves. It is about freedom, the freedom of people to choose how to live their own lives. It is about tolerance of minorities – and, sadly, those who live and work in our countryside are minorities here today. And above all it is about listening to and respecting the views of other people of which you may personally disapprove . . .

Many of you spend your lives living and working with animals. You see birth and death at close quarters. It is you who take the hard decisions, you who bear the responsibilities day in, day out, and do the sheer hard work. It is an irony that this rally, composed as it is of people who know, love and live among animals, should be the target of abuse and vilification from those who claim to love animals but seldom have any practical knowledge of or direct responsibility for caring for them. The irresponsible seem to feel free and qualified to tell the responsible that they are – and I quote – barbaric sadists and perverts. Well – there are an awful lot of perverts in front of me at the moment . . .

Tonight this park will empty. We will, all of us, be making our way home to all parts of the nation. We will go back to care for the animals and the countryside and its wildlife, of which we have been guardians for generations.

Don't forget us, or what we have done today, because we have made history. The countryside has come to London to speak out for freedom – and many from the towns and cities who understand our fears have stood here with us today. Today our voice has been one of calm reason. But make no mistake – the countryside is angry.

I hope that we are not on the eve of a battle. We do not want one. But if there is one, the countryside will fight back, and the countryside will win. To all those of you who have just given part of your lives to be here in Hyde Park, and particularly to those who have marched from all ends of our country, the best words that I can end with are those of another countryman, our greatest writer, addressing a minority on the eve of another battle, which was won against all the odds:

From this day to the ending of the world,
But we in it shall be remembered;
We few, we happy few, we band of brothers;
For he today who sheds his blood with me
Shall be my brother; be he ne'er so vile
This day shall gentle his condition:
And gentlemen in England, now a-bed
Shall think themselves accurs'd they were not
    here,
And hold their manhoods cheap whiles any
    speaks
That fought with us upon . . . .
             the tenth of July 1997.

As she came to the middle of the great passage from *Henry V,*

Baroness Mallalieu let go of her sheaf of notes. But she carried on without hesitation, finishing to a storm of applause.

Other speeches followed, and because the programme was running late, several distinguished speakers had to be stood down. Then singing broke out: 'Jerusalem', 'John Peel' (with the *view hall*OOOOOOOs held out to a ridiculous length), and other favourites. Now at last, in a final burst of defiance, Andrew Sallis turned up the amplifiers, and with a proper lead from the stage, 120,000 voices swung into a few terrific choruses. When the crowd waved their song sheets aloft, it looked as though a sudden storm had swept the ocean of faces into a mass of flying white horses. By then the sense of achievement and the euphoria were so great that, after barely three hours, people felt they had had their money's worth, and began to drift away.

All along the Parks Agency and the police had expressed their anxiety that the rally should not end abruptly, giving rise to a sudden mass exodus. To the organisers' question, 'How do we persuade people to hang around, if we cannot entertain them?' there had been no sensible answer. Yet in the end people began to move off by the hundred rather than by the thousand, and no bad crush developed. The only serious block came when two antis chained themselves to an escalator in Green Park tube station, and machinery had to be shut down until they were barred off. Out in the BFSS office Peter Voute had two scares – one when a twelve-year-old boy was reported missing from a coach (he later reappeared), and the other when a call came from Exmoor, saying that two fifteen-year-old girls were not on board the coach which had returned from London (they too were found in due course).

By four o'clock the Cavalry Parade Ground was almost empty, and the departure of the crowd revealed one final surprise. The litter-pickers who came on were the very team that had cleaned up after the Gay Pride rally the weekend before. Then, they had found a disgusting mess, which took them days to sort out. Now, when the country people departed, they were astonished to find that there was nothing to pick up.

The party from Caithness and Sutherland, who had travelled all night to arrive at 7.30 that morning, set out for home at 4pm and were back in Inverness by 4.30 am on Friday. David Horborough, a ghillie at Syre Lodge on the River Naver, and his friends still had nearly two hours to go: the worst part of the trip was the last, when they met thick fog. Their driver, Donald Bruce, was so tired that they kept having to give him short breaks and walk him up and down to prevent him falling asleep. Finally reaching base at 6.15 am, Horborough went to bed, slept till mid-day, and was back on his beat of the Naver for the afternoon. He felt that the excursion was thoroughly worthwhile, not least because he had met 'a helluva people' he had not seen for a long time.

Afterwards Michael Parker, though greatly relieved that everything had passed off successfully, was maddened by the way the BBC, crawling with political correctness, had handled the rally in its Archers radio serial. For weeks the programme had blathered on about the Gay Pride rally, with numerous references to the fact that Sean, publican at the Cat and Fiddle in Ambridge, was off to Hyde Park on the great day. Not once did the story of ordinary country folk mention the greatest countryside event in living memory – until, goaded by listeners' complaints, a few lame references were added after the event.

CHAPTER NINE

Aftermath

The BFSS had no doubt that the rally was a rip-roaring success. Over a thousand letters of thanks and congratulation poured in from members all over the country, many bearing donations. The voice of the countryside had been heard as never before. People spoke of having crossed a watershed, of having entered a new era. The Society's leaders were invigorated, and filled with fresh determination to continue the fight for their cause.

The march organisers, equally, were elated at the response which their initiative had evoked. Charles Mann had been planning to close down his office immediately after the rally, but demands for further action were so insistent that he decided to keep it open for the foreseeable future. His main problem, now, was not to goad people into speaking up for country sports, but to prevent them resorting to violence or civil unrest in attempts to disable the Foster bill.

In 1995, writing in the *Evening Standard* about the rural origins of his fellow-author Dennis Potter, the television playwright Ian Curteis had made a crucial point:

Not one, but two, civilisations live on these islands. There is the intensely metropolitan one – smart, fashionable, somewhat rootless, highly competitive, only about seventy years old – which dominates our media, particularly broadcasting. And there is the far older one, its roots outside London, with entirely different values, provincial in the way Shakespeare was; a civilisation that gave birth to most of our great literature, music and art, with a far stronger sense of continuity, history and the countryside.

Until recently, those two civilisations have lived more or less in harmony, tolerating each other. But now suddenly the new urban civilisation has become more aggressive, and is seeking to trample its elder partner out of existence. The peasants' revolt of 1997 showed how ill-judged the attempt may be, and gave a hint of the consequences that may follow unless compromises are worked out. Many people felt – or at any rate hoped – that the sheer size of the crowd at the rally gave the Government a shock, and that after such a show of potential strength the Labour administration will, as one man put it, 'stop one pace short of treading on a landmine.'

As for the core marchers: they, too, came away from the rally elated. Some said they could have walked on water, others that they could have gone through fire without noticing it. Mary Holt 'could easily have walked to Cairo,' and several of the Welsh remarked that if David Jones had told them to march straight out of the Hyde Park and on to Paris, they would have done so. June Moon, from Cornwall, was scandalised and delighted when a burly Welshman swept her off her feet. 'He picked me up like a baby!' she exclaimed indignantly. 'And I *am* ten stone.'

Then, inevitably, after wild parties on bus or train during the journey home, there came a feeling of immense let-down – a sense that for two or three weeks a select band had lived on a level of effort and emotion which they might never reach again. After such an adventure, ordinary life seemed hum-drum.

Several felt guilty that they had got too much credit merely for walking. 'It was after all so very easy,' wrote Henry (Legs) Hudson. 'Twenty miles a day, with rest days? My little sister could do that.' The praise, he reckoned, should have gone to the organisers:

> Anybody can plod down a road, but only a few could have put this together. They didn't get the parties every night, and couldn't switch off and chat in the daytime. But that was where the brilliance and dedication really lay.

Tony, hero of the Cornish march, reckoned he would never forget the experience of Hyde Park, which made him 'more optimistic for the future' and reaffirmed for him that 'country people in general display good, old-fashioned values of kindness, honesty and decency which are sadly lacking in our society today.' James Allen, a seventeen-year-old, had no inhibitions about answering what *he* got out of the march – 'Women!' But his mother reckoned that her son had benefited tremendously: 'He developed a wonderful sense of humour and made a new bunch of friends who will be friends for life. He has learnt what the word "commitment" means, and is a far better young man for taking part.'

Richard Markham found that the march had made him 'more open-minded about other people's thoughts and livelihoods.' John Morris came away with 'an increased awareness of the bond which binds true countrymen throughout the nation,' and to Mark Naisby, the Highlander who never gave old whisky a chance to go off, 'The whole campaign showed that there is an army out there. Yes, it is a rural army, and if need be it will be mobilised again, and in larger numbers.'

Let the last word rest with a Scottish investment banker who was so impressed by the performance of the core marchers that, as a token of his personal gratitude, he sent all 136 of them a bottle of fine whisky.

The Countryside Song

by
George Bowyer

Oh, what a pity!
Oh, what a shame!
Someone is trying to ban country sports again.

But *we* know the glory of the countryside,
The glory of the beasts there that swim and run and fly.
It's us who preserve the woodlands, the rivers and the hills,
And if they'll only let us, then we always will.

Because we are the guardians, the keepers of the land,
And we know what would happen if country sports were banned.
Who would replace the care and management that we provide?
It would mean the raping of our countryside.

Because the environment needs management each and every day,
And we are the ones who do the work and we are the ones who pay.
Landscape and wildlife of all sorts, we owe them all to country
sports, we do,
We owe them all to country sports.

We know the glory of the countryside,
The glory of the beasts there that swim and run and fly.
It's us who preserve the woodlands, the rivers and the hills,
And if they'll only let us, then we always will.

The Countryside Song

And if the Antis ban us, you can be quite sure
That they won't bother to do the work we've done before;
But the trees will still need planting, hedges must still be laid,
The moors will still need burning, and the bills must still be paid!

Their lack of understanding is a national disgrace,
For what they would destroy could never be replaced.
For landscape and wildlife of all sorts, the future lies with country
   sports, it does, The future lies with country sports.

We know the glory of the countryside,
The glory of the beasts there that swim and run and fly.
It's us who preserve the woodlands, the rivers and the hills,
And if they'll only let us, then we always will.

We are the guardians and the keepers of the land,
And we know what would happen if country sports were banned.
For landscape and wildlife of all sorts, the future lies with country
   sports, it does,
The future lies with country sports.

Core Marchers

NOTE *The majority of the marchers listed here walked the full distance, but lack of time forced some to join in for only part of the route. The official ruling was that no one joining after 27 June – the start-date in Wales – could be classed as a core marcher, but here I have given everyone the benefit of the doubt.*

CALDBECK AND COLDSTREAM TO LONDON

14 June 1997 to 9 July 1997
LEADERS   John Harrison and Edward Tate

Richard Akrigg
Lucy Akrigg
Ian Alexander
Diana Barker
Anthony Bealby
Gary Bell
Wilson Boow
George Bowyer
Dave Brearley
Zara Brett
David Brown
Archie Clapton
Joanna Clapton
Dave Clement

Paul Crofts
Derek Cross
Suzannah Elms
George Grant
Mary Holt
Henry Hudson
Rowena Hudson
Peter Jones-Davis
Richard Markham
Alastair McDiarmid
Sarah Morley
John Morris
Mark Naisby
Carl Naisby

Michael Nicholson
Nathan Oldham
Reggie Purbrick
David Simms
Paul Steel
Martin Thornton
Dick Tonks
Richard Tyacke
Shaun Vickers
Richard Wakeham
William Wakeham
John Walls
Greig Watts
Michael Woodhouse

Core Marchers

CORNWALL TO LONDON

22 June 1997 to 9 July 1997
ORGANISERS   David and Jo Latham
LEADER   Brian Webber

Jackie Alway	Peter Earnshaw	Hilary Pascoe
Michael Alway	James Hill	Shirley Pascoe
David Aubin	David Lear	Jeremy Scott-Bolton
Tim Badden	Caroline Lynch	Katherine Sealy
Kathryn Bailey	Graham Marks	James Sealy
Alethea Bick	Neil Mathieson	Mark Selway
Martyn Blackmore	Jonathan McCulloch	Sam Taylor
Mike Brill	June Moon	Alexander Thavenot
Nick Bryant	David Neal	Peter Webb
Angelique Cheshire	Robin Nicholls	Paul Williams
Simon Copperwait	Norman Osborne	Anthony Winchcombe
David Daly	Amie Pascoe	

MACHYNLLETH AND ST CLEARS TO LONDON

27 June 1997 to 9 July 1997
LEADER   David Jones
SOUTH WALES ORGANISERS   Adrian Simpson, Simon Hart

James Allen	John Bulkeley	Charles Frampton
Diane Barker	Jan Collins	Matthew Garfield
Greg Barker	Dylan Davies	Gemma Green
David Barber	Alan Day	Gail Greenhouse
Gary Barber	Neville Edwards	Charles Gundry
Tom Barrow	Dylan Evans	Simon Hall
Geoff Bow	Emma Farquhar	Jamie Hanks
Nick Brunt	Joe Folder	Ian Haynes
Ian Bucknell	Alex Ford	Ian Hawkins

137

Steven Hill
Tony Hinde
Darren Hughes
Gavin Hughes
Michael Hughes
Roger Hughes
Michael Ings
Austin James
Richard Jones
Ednyfed Jones
Jessica Kingsley
Michael Kitchen

Tom Leeke
Richard Lovett
Chris Maiden
David Morgan
Sue Morgan
Andrea Richards
Stephen Robbins
Nicola Roberts
Roy Savage
Tasha Stevens
Rupert Sturgis
Paul Tate

Huw Thomas
Anna Turner
Karen Turner
Heather Tylor
George Wade
Brian Warfield
Gary Whelband
David Williams
Richard Williams
Mal Williams
John Wingfield
Kirstie Wood

THE MARCHES OFFICE

The office was set up and run by Charles and Chipps Mann and Sam Butler. The volunteers who manned it included Karen Abel-Smith, Liz Acland, Luke Annaly, Jillie Barrow, Amanda Butler, Julie Delamain, Catherine Flach, Charlotte Heber-Percy, Prue Hornby, Jeanie Keyser, Olivia Townshend and Liz Wills.

Acknowledgements

I should like to thank the many core marchers who responded to my appeal for information. I do not list all their names here, because they appear in the roll of honour above. I apologise to those who returned their questionnaire but do not feature in the text: often several people made the same point or mentioned the same event, and it would have been tedious to repeat every reference.

For information, ideas and help in general, I am particularly grateful to the following: Liz Acland, Tom Barrow, George Bowyer, Dave Brearley, Sam Butler, Simon Clarke, Dave Clement, Amanda Courtney, Posy Coutts, Mary Eames, Richard Edmonds, Alan Evershed, Pamela Faulks, Vic Gardner, Janet George, Robin Hanbury-Tenison, John Harrison, Simon Hart, Charlotte Heber-Percy, Mary Holt, John Howard-Jones, David Jones, Pip Jones, David Krassner, David and Jo Latham, David Lear, Baroness Mallalieu, Charles and Chipps Mann, Mark Miller Mundy, June Moon, John Morris, Michael Parker, Amie Pascoe, Reggie Purbrick, Andrew Sallis, Adrian Simpson, Edward Tate, Barry Todhunter, Heather Tylor, Peter Voute, Peter Webb, Brian Webber.

For their help in providing photographs, I am grateful to Mike Brill, Sam Butler, Dave Clement, *The Countryman's Weekly*, *Horse & Hound*, David Lear, Chipps Mann, Kathryn Pearn and Peter Webb.

139

Index

141

Index

Index

Index

Index

Index

Index

Index

Index